भर्तृहरिकृत श्रृंगारशतक

Bhartrhari's

One Hundred Verses on Love

भर्तृहरिकृत श्रृंगारशतक

Bhartrhari's

One Hundred Verses on Love

Harsha V. Dehejia

MOTILAL BANARSIDASS
PUBLICATIONS

Bhartrhari's Harsha V. Dehejia

First Edition : Delhi, 2020

ISBN : 978-81-94-2438-6-1

Published by

Motilal Banarsidass Publications

93, Shyam Lal Marg, Darya Ganj, New Delhi-110002 (India)

mlbd@mlbd.com

Printed by Anvi Composers

Translation

Sudha and Harsha Dehejia

Texts

L.G. Vinjhe, *Bhartrharikrit Shatakatrayi*,
Nirnaya Sagar Prakashan, Mumbai, 1908
Purohit Gopi Nath, *The Shatakas of Bhartrhari*
Bharatiya Kala Prakashan, New Delhi, 2010
Greg Bailey, *Love Lyrics of Bhartrhari*
Clay Sanskrit Library, New York University Press, New York, 2005

Design

Shrinidhi Sridhar

Fonts

Garamond, Remachine, Mogra

Devnagari

Seema Jadhav of Achyut Palav Calligraphy

Art Credit

Sketches: Akshay Ameria, Ujjain
Watercolour: Kalashri Kantichandra Bharadwaj, Indore

Pre-press Production

Reproscan, Mumbai

Dedicated to the women in Bhartrhari's *Shringara* Shataka

Whether slandered or pampered
demure or defiant, with loving or sidelong glances
with eyes that rival the lotus,
her brows that dance to every emotion
with a face that puts the moon to shame
inviting or ignoring the male gaze
neither Madana nor mankind can capture this woman
no poet can contain her, no words can fully reach her
for she stands secure and self-assured
enigmatic and mysterious
in the many intricacies of *shringara*.

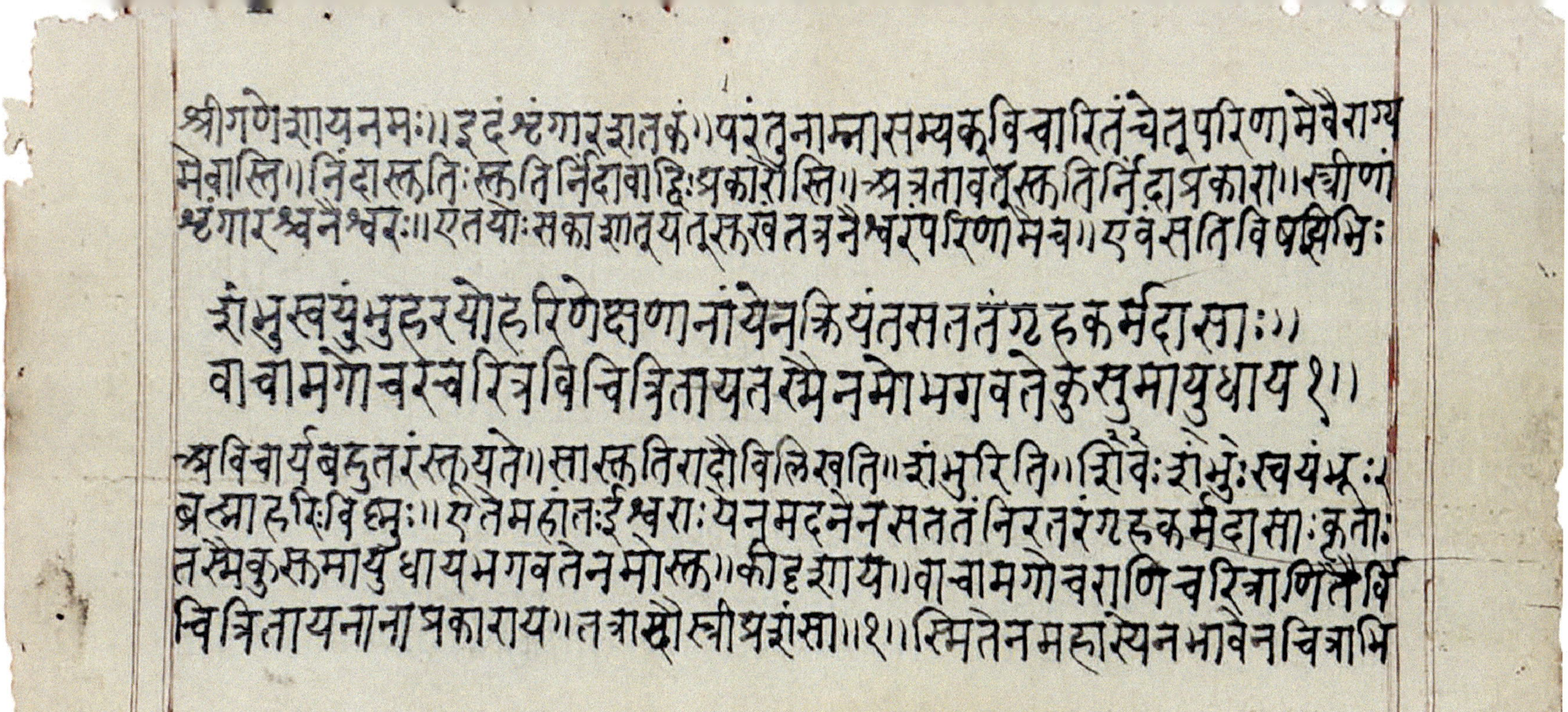

श्रीगणेशाय नमः ॥ इदं शृंगारशतकं ॥ परं तु नाम्ना सम्यक् विचारितं चेत् परिणामे वैराग्य
मेवास्ति ॥ निंदास्तुतिः स्तुतिनिंदा वा द्विःप्रकारोस्ति ॥ अत्र तावत् स्तुतिर्निंदाप्रकारा ॥ स्त्रीणां
शृंगारश्च नैश्वर्यः ॥ एतयोः सकाशात् यत् सुखं तत्र नैश्वर्यपरिणामे च ॥ एवं सति विपश्चिद्भिः

शंभुस्वयंभुहरयो हरिणेक्षणानां येनाक्रियंत सततं गृहकर्मदासाः ॥
वाचामगोचरचरित्रविचित्रिताय तस्मै नमो भगवते कुसुमायुधाय १ ॥

अविचार्य बहुतरं स्तूयते ॥ सा स्तुतिरादौ विलिखति ॥ शंभुरिति ॥ शिवः शंभुः स्वयंभूः
ब्रह्मा हरिर्विष्णुः ॥ एते महांतः ईश्वराः येन मदनेन सततं निरंतरं गृहकर्मदासाः कृताः
तस्मै कुसुमायुधाय भगवते नमोस्तु ॥ कीदृशाय ॥ वाचामगोचराणि चरित्राणि तैर्वि
विचित्रिताय नानाप्रकाराय ॥ तत्रासौ स्त्रीप्रशंसा ॥ १ ॥ स्मितेन महास्येन भावेन चित्राभि

Mangalacharan, Bhartrhari's Shringara Shataka, Western India, 18th century
Bhandarkar Oriental Research Institute, Pune

Kama and Rati, Rajasthan, 18th century

9 Bhartrhari, The Poet and The Poetry.

Harsha V. Dehejia

When one tries to write about an ancient poet from a modern book, namely trying to glean something of Bhartrhari from the *Shatakam* Trayi that is available to us today, one is dealing with many distortions created by the passage of time as well as the editor of the book. To start with the editor has established a chronology by starting with the *niti shataka* and ending with the *vairagya shataka* and placing the *shringara shataka* in the middle.

This could lead to many false and even troublesome conclusions: that this is the chronology intended by the author and even more that the author feels that in life *niti* must precede *shringara* and that it be followed by *vairagya*, relegating *shringara* to an intermediate position. Even more it could lead to an erroneous justification that *vairagya* must supercede *shringara* and that it is the ultimate end of life. Is it possible that Bhartrhari wrote the *vairagya shataka* first and then the *shringara shataka*? Could *shringara* be the main end of lifefor Bhartrhari? Is it also possible that he wrote the verses randomly without any intended pattern?

Finally, could Bhartrhari have implied that *niti*, *shringara* and *vairagya* should be synchronous and not in separate compartments? Thus it is best to suspend the chronology that the editor has imposed on us. Indian thought, like the Indian *thali* of food, asserts a seamless synchronicity, rather than dichotomies and a piece meal approach. The three, namely *niti*, *shringara* and *vairagya* must be held together as a whole.

The second problem when working with a modern book of an ancient poet is the question of interpolation: are we sure that all the verses are indeed that of Bhartrhari?

When we convert an oral tradition to a written one the problem of interpolation is all too common. One has seen this with poetry and even wisdom traditions like that of Surdas. There are many hand written manuscripts of Bhartrhari's poetry but even there, there is no consistency, when it comes to the number of verses and their chronology, which again suggests that the conversion of Bhartrhari's oral verses to text may have been done in many different places and supported by a variety of patrons and created by varied scribes.

In the absence of historical records there are many speculations about Bhartrhari the person. From all accounts he probably lived in the 4th or the 6th century CE in Ujjain and that he may have been a brother of king Vikramaditya. It is fair to assume that he followed Kalidasa and preceded Amaru. Was he the same person who was the grammarian philosopher who wrote the Vakyapadiya? Was he a Buddhist monk? Did his wife betray him? All of these questions have been asked and even answered by some, but we shall not enter into this dimly lit space as it unproductive to our inquiry. As connoisseurs of poetry we by-pass even historical information as we are interested only in poetry and not the poet, as this is the hallmark of aesthetics or *saundarya mimamsa* in the Indian tradition. We take on the white light of the sun rather than grope in shadowy light. We delight in celebrating anonymous works of art, whether in word or stone, paper or mud wall, temple or palace and therefore we need not worry about the historicity of Bhartrhari beyond a certain point.

Finally, there are as many speculations about his death as there are about his life. One account is fascinating not because of its historicity but of its mystical details. Apparently in a small village near Alwar is Siriska where in a jungle there are seven chhatris. According to local residents they represent the *samadhi sthanas*, the final resting place of Bhartrhari, the six where he took samadhi and the seventh where there is votive lamp burning all day and night where he will come and perform his last *samadhi*! Such and other stories need not detain us for our task is to examine his poetry and poesy where idle historical speculations hinder rather than help in our academic pursuit of the aesthetics of Bhartrhari's poetry.

Bhartrahri's *shringara trayi* occupies an important place in the annals of Sanskrit literature for many reasons. While *shringara rasa* was probably enunciated in Prakrit

in times pre-historic and even before his time as in Hala's Saptasati, Bhartrhari was perhaps the first poet who broke the norm of not using Sanskrit for romantic literature. In his time Sanskrit was the language of the nobility and of the royalty, it was the language of liturgy, the language of philosophic discourse and of our wisdom traditions and which was courtly and not pedestrian and spoken by men and not women. It was the language of the gods in the world of mankind, such was its rarefied stature. Bhartrhari turns his back on these norms and conventions and launches into *shringara* in classical Sanskrit. If we accept Ujjain as the city where Bhartrhari lived and even more if we read Sudhir Kakkad's beautiful fiction Devil Take Love, we will be in an enchanted space, where courtesans reveled in romantic environments and poets sang songs in Sanskrit of clandestine romantic encounters, even as wine flowed and aromatic nights were celebrated, then we may be privy to the times in which Bhartrhari lived and loved for a brief but delightful moment of historical fiction. While not adding academic substance to Bhartrhari's poetry it certainly gives an interesting, even though fictional, backdrop.

Bhartrhari's language is direct and almost to the point of being terse and it has none of the lyrical quality of later Sanskrit love poetry. He prefers to avoid metaphors and uses words with a certain directness. His words are almost arrow like, they leave him and hit the target, and make their point. They are *marmik*, almost personal. It is as if Bhartrhari is describing his own personal experiences. Within the orbit of a few lines he expresses, as it were, his own dilemmas of life, between *shringara* and *vairagya*. As Aklujkar states, "I am not aware of any other Sanskrit poet in whose case we come so close to believing that a personal experience is finding expression in his compositions."[1]Bhartrhari does not romanticise *shringara*, but instead portrays the many dilemmas of celebrating both *kamana* and *shringara*, desire and romance. Miller writes that, "The poet cannot choose between asceticism and worldly indulgence because he finds them equally attractive and equally deficient."[2]He undermines all concepts of absolute values in almost a zen like fashion. He fractures any kind of absolute vision of truth or ultimate reality which has shades of Buddhist thought in it. *Shringara* for him must embody *vairagya* and in *vairagya*, the excitement of amorous pleasures ends for him in a sigh of pain. Are there vague flickers of *vama*-Tantra here?

Bhartrhari maintains a tension between sensuality and spirituality, between joyously embracing this world and renouncing it. At one moment Bhartrhari is rapturous about the exalted state of a loving couple when he compares perfect love to the *ardhanari* where there is no duality and no space between the lover and the beloved; at the very next moment he caitions us that if such is not the case then one must be an ascetic like Shiva. If it is to be *shringara* it should be so absolute as in the *ardhanarishvara* Shiva, leaving no room for the duality of the lover and the loved. If it is to be *vairagya*, it should be so firm as to rival that of Shiva.Unfortunately, neither seems to be within the reach of human beings.They seem to be condemned to an in between state of poison filled delirium.

He does not describe the locale of the romantic interaction, there are no *havelis* or *nikunjas*, no flower garlands or aromatic unguents, no *pranay mandapas* or moonlit rendezvous. Equally he does not bother to depict *shangar* or the adornments of the *nayika*, there is no description of her clothes or jewelry. like necklace or anklets, flowers or garlands. Aklujar suggests that Sanskrit of his time was a literary language not frequently employed to speak of worldly objects of adornments like jewelry.[3]

Bhartrhari clearly suggests that physical ornaments have no role to play in a woman's beauty when she has a face to rival the moon, eyes that make mockery of lotuses, complexion eclipsing the lustre of gold, thick tresses that shame the black bee, breasts like elephant's swelling temples. However he does refer to "white jasmine about to bloom in her hair, sandal paste mixed with saffron on her body." In a telling verse Bhartrhari says "moral conduct is a gem that crown's the rest.". Thus the glitter of gold, the radiance of precious stones and the shimmer of silk does not have any room in Bhartrhari's poetry. Some have suggested that in his time there were probably no ornaments that we know today and which are an essential part of a nayika whether in poetry or painting.

One way of understanding Bhartrhari is to try and come to terms with his sense of time. The serene flow of circular time which is the quintessence of much of Sanskrit literature is absent in Bhartrhari's *shringara shataka*. Instead, blocking and release, where time does not flow but jumps, it expands but then suddenly telescopes, all of which creates syntactic and semantic suspense, and is perhaps a vision of his mind.[4]His poetry was meant to be read and spoken and not sung or danced and in the brevity of a couple of lines it presents a romantic interaction in its bare bone fashion. Assuming

for a moment that our Bhartrhari the poet is the same as Bhartrhari the grammarian, it is worth recounting this line from the *Vakyapadiya*: "...if speech were to disappear light would go out. Speech informed awareness is the foundation of all knowledge, arts and artisinal practices.[5] It is quite obvious that in his time the *shatakam* was to be orally spoken and recited and that even after it was transformed into a manuscript, it is the human voice that gives Bhartrhari's verses a reality. It is the human voice, with texture and intonation, with feeling and desire, that makes the *shringara* verses of Bhartrhari come alive. This is true of Bhartrhari more than any other romantic Sanskrit poet. *Shringara* normally is best expressed through *abhinaya*, through *mudras*, through gestures and the human voice and it is the human voice more than the rest that is the best messenger of *shringara* for Bhartrhari. This is also borne out in the metres of his verses. While he seems to mix different metres in most of his verses, the words seems to flow in a cadence like a waterfall rather flow like a river. He also uses alliteration and symmetrical phrasing and it has been suggested that some of his verses are almost iconic, resembling the *ardhanarisvara*, where *purusha* and *prakriti*, come together.

Bhartrhari does not shy away from offering his own, often sarcastic, comments on the appropriateness of the romantic behavior. He takes on a magisterial role, passing judgement on the appropriateness or otherwise of a particular romantic attitude. One feels that he was an observer or participant in the romantic interlude and one feels even from the written text that Bhartrhari is presiding over the celebration of his verses and is not just a distant observer.

Richard Gombrich writes: "Bhartrihari is idiosyncratic within the tradition of Sanskrit poetry, a quality that has endeared him to Western readers. Another commentator Siegfried Lehnard writes: Bhartrihari's personality appears much more clearly in his work than is the case with the majority of classical Indian poets. It is characteristic of Bhartrihari's love poems that they do not contain the usual lyrical scenes. The poet's pronounced intellectual leanings are unmistakable."[6]

Bhartrhari was an iconoclast and came before the Bhagavata Purana and this explains some of the sharpness, leanness and aggressiveness of his poetry. Bhartrhari's *shringara* is without *bhakti* and we shall return to this later. The *dashama skanda* of the Bhagavata

was a turning point in the history of *shringara rasa*. Krishna's presence, and later Radha's position in *shringara*, assures Krishna poetry, and all later Radha Krishna poetry, of a distinct *madhurya* or sweetness. In Krishna poetry the gopis and Radha represent all women in love, there is no particularity but universality, not one gopi but all gopis, while Bhartrhari's *nayikas* are individuals. *Shringara rasa* was a stepping stone to *shringara bhakti* and the *madhurya* that Krishna expresses through his words and actions is a form of *jnana* or knowledge. It goes without saying that Bhartrhari was not touched by Krishna *shringara* and therefore there is no element of *madhura bhakti* in his *shringara*.

It is also noteworthy that Bhartrhari does not portray *viraha* or the *virahini* in the *shringara shatakam* which is so much a part of later Sanskrit romantic poetry. The Bhagavata and the Gita Govinda sing about viraha in evocative terms and Bhabudutta's Rasmanjari and Ritikavya is profuse with descriptions and classifications of the *virahini*. *Viraha* has an important role both aesthetically and metaphysically. Bhartrhari does not enter this terrain at all. It is viraha, either impending or actual, that chastens *shringara* and creates *shringara bhakti*. The *gopis* in the Bhagavata and Radha in the Gita Govinda internalise Krishna and despite the pangs of *viraha* there is total and joyous surrender and no sense of bitterness or despondency that one sees in Bhartrhari's *shringara*. Bhartrhari's *nayikas* are strikingly different from those of Kalidasa and Amaru, two authors of many, who have celebrated *shringara* rasa in Sanskrit. She is self-aware and assured, defiant and not demure, negotiating the many paths of love on her own terms and above all upholding the dignity of *kamana*. She is both *kamini* and *sundari*, sensuously attractive and romantically inviting and of all her physical endowments her eyes were the most evocative. Those eyes would sometimes stare and at other times invite, they would wink with satire and at other times smile and laugh, they would admonish and admire, they would have tears of joy and sorrow but above all they would be eyes that speak the *mantra* of *shringara* and it is with her eyes that were a window to her mind that she negotiated the many and intricate paths of love. Here are Bhartrhari's words when it comes to the eyes of a nayika:

dancing eyes, sidelong glances, doe like eyes, flickering glances,
glance like that of an arrow, restless eyes, dancing serpentine eyebrows,
lotus eyes, intoxicated eyes.

In paying so much attention to glances Bhartrhari is emphasising subtle but cultured communication and he presupposes a society in which language of the eyes is important and it speaks of the cognoscenti that is cultured and cultivated who can traverse the many paths of abhinaya and do not have to rely on words. Bhartrhari's *nayikas* are never in a state of *vairagya*, they are forever sensuous and an object of the male gaze. *Vairagya* is for the male protagonist which possibly suggests that the poet is also the protagonist.

As one leaves reading and experiencing the *shringara shatakam* one cannot but be impressed by Bhartrhari's mastery of the language, his forthright expressions, his unabashed sensuality, but at the same time one senses that there is a *vairagi* hiding within the poet, a *fakir* whispering to a *kavi*, a sage beckoning to a pleasure seeking king. Notwithstanding this, Bhartrhari remains a poet to be reckoned with, his poetry is a beacon in the annals of *shringara rasa kavya*, and is an important landmark to those who traverse the highway of Indian poetry. And perchance we reach his *samadhi* we shall carry flowers that will whisper that there once was a king who dared to love but who also could not resist the call of renunciation.

End Notes

1 Ashok Aklujkar, paper presented at Shangar & Shringara, Mumbai, 1995
2 Barbara Stoller Miller
3 ibid
4 Toward a History of Kavya Literature,ed Bronner, Shulmanm, Tubb Oxford University Press, 2018 p. 66-67
5 Sidney Pollock, The Language of Gods in the World of Men, Columbia University Press, 2000, p. 82
6 Richard Gombrich, p. 18

Paintings by

Kalashri Kantichandra Bharadwaj

Kama and Rati, Central India, 12th century

2 Bhartrihari, A Poet For All Times

Bibek Debroy

There were many great poets in Sanskrit. In any list of great Sanskrit poets, Bharthari/ Bhartrihari will feature at the top. I mean Shatakatrayam, not Vakyapadiya. Alas, we know little about Bhartrihari's life. What we know, whether it is in James Tod's accounts or Sudhir Kakar's fiction, is the stuff of legends. But Bharthari is not the stuff of legends. These terse verses are perennial and delight us even today. As examples, take the following. These sentiments are universal in their resonance.

या चिन्तयामि सततं मयि सा विरक्ता
साप्यन्यमिच्छति जनं स जनोऽन्यसक्तः।
अस्मत्कृते च परिशुष्यति काचिदन्या
धिक् तां च तं च मदनं च इमां च मां च ॥
लभेत सिकतासु तैलमपि यत्नतः पीडतन्

पिबेच्च मृगतृष्णिकासु सलिलं पिपासार्दितः।
कदाचिदपि पर्यटन्शशविषाणमासादयेन्
न तु प्रतिनिविष्टमूर्खजनचित्तमाराधयेत् ॥

केयूराणि न भूषयन्ति पुरुषं हारा न चन्द्रोज्ज्वला
न स्नानं न विलेपनं न कुसुमं नालङ्कृता मूर्धजाः।
वाण्येका समलङ्करोति पुरुषं या संस्कृता धार्यते
क्षीयन्ते खलु भूषणानि सततं वाग्भूषणं भूषणम् ॥

The three examples I have given are from Nitisataka. Many verses from Nitisataka are familiar to students, because they have entered text-books, and are also familiar to others, though people may not necessarily know these were composed by Bhartrihari. However, my personal take is that the verses in Srngarasataka and Vairagyasataka take us to an altogether different plane of poetry. Especially in this day and age, literature is often interpreted as the written word, with a script and a medium, digital or non-digital, through which that written word finds form. But literature cannot be delinked from language and language is about the spoken word, not the written. Language is not what the eyes read, but what the mouth speaks and what the ears hear. Language is about sound, cadence, metre and rhythm. Any act of translation transcreates, it cannot hope to exactly replicate the original. Translation is easier from prose. It becomes difficult for poetry, where a successful translator also has to be a bit of a poet. Translation becomes more difficult for a language like Sanskrit. It becomes exceedingly difficult for a poet like Bhartrihari, where words have double meanings and verses are terse.

केशाः संयमिनः श्रुतेरपि परं पारं गते लोचने
अन्तर्वक्त्रमपि स्वभावशुचिभिः कीर्णं द्विजानां गणैः ।
मुक्तानां सतताधिवासरुचिरौ वक्षोजकुम्भाविमा
वित्थं तन्वि! वपुः प्रशान्तमपि ते क्षोभं करोत्येव नः ॥
गुरुणा स्तनभारेण मुखचन्द्रेण भास्वता ।
शनैश्चराभ्यां पादाभ्यां रेजे ग्रहमयीव सा ॥
मुखेय चन्द्रकान्तेन महानीलैः शिरोरुहैः ।
पाणिभ्यां पद्मरागाभ्यां रेजे रत्नमयीव सा ॥

Let me give three verses from Srngarasataka to illustrate the point.(on the left)

I am also fascinated by the different metres (*chandas*) that feature in Bhartrihari's verses. Beauty of literature and language apart, Bhartrihari's verses have pedagogical value for students wishing to learn about Sanskrit prosody. Let me give four examples from Srngarasataka. The actual list is much longer. (on the right)

अनुष्टुभ्
नूनमाज्ञाकरस्तस्याः सुभ्रुवो मकरध्वजः ।
यतस्तन्नेत्रसञ्चारसूचितेषु प्रवर्तते ॥
वसन्ततिलका
एताश्चलद्वलयसंहतिमेखलोत्थ
झंकारनूपुरपराजितराजहंस्यः।
कुर्वन्ति कस्य न मनो विवशं तरुण्यो
वित्रस्तमुग्धहरिणीसदृशैः कटाक्षैः ॥
शिखरिणी
कृशः काणः खञ्जः श्रवणरहितः पुच्छविकलो
व्रणी पूयक्लिन्नः कृमिकुलशतैरावृततनुः ।
क्षुधाक्षामो जीर्णः पिङ्गरककपालार्पितगलः
शुनीमन्वेति श्वा! हतमपि च हन्त्येव मदनः ॥
शार्दूलविक्रीडित
आवासः किलञ्चितस्य दयिताः पार्श्वे विलासालसाः
कर्णे कोकिलकामिनीकलरवः स्मेरो लतामण्डपः ।
गोष्ठी सत्कविभिः समं कतिपयैः सेव्याः सितांशो कराः
केषाञ्चित्सुखयन्ति धन्यहृदयं चैत्रे विचित्राः क्षपाः ॥

भ्रान्तं देशमनेकदुर्गविषमं प्राप्तं न किञ्चित्फलम्
त्यक्त्वा जातिकुलाभिमानमुचितं सेवा कृता निष्फला ।
भुक्तं मानविवर्जितं परगृहेष्वाशङ्कया काकवत्
तृष्णे जृम्भसि पापकर्मपिशुने नाद्यापि सन्तुष्यसि ॥
वलीभिर्मुखमाक्रान्तं पलितेनाङ्कितं शिरः ।
गात्राणि शिथिलायन्ते तृष्णैका तरुणायते ॥
एकाकी निःस्पृहःशान्तःपाणिपात्रो दिगम्बरः ।
कदा शम्भो भविष्यामि कर्मनिर्मूलनक्षमः ॥

A *kavi* is a person who is wise. That word conveys a meaning much deeper than that of a mere poet. There is playfulness with not just the content, but also the form, of the Srngarasataka verses. Irrespective of the legends about Bhartrihari, with or without King Vikramaditya, Vairagyasataka is the wise person's take. As before, I will give three examples. The second of these has always reminded me of Adi Shankaracharya's Bhajagovindam and I have wondered whether Adi Shankaracharya was familiar with Bhartrihari. In any event, we should be familiar with Bhartrihari. Bhartrihari's poetry has been translated in the past. It will continue to be translated. This is a treasure and legacy that is perennial, for generations to savour. I have visited the Bhartrihari caves in Ujjain and the Bhartrihari temple in Sariska. But the Bhartrihari legacy of Satakatrayam is something I keep visiting again and again, and so should everyone else.

Kama on a composite elephant, Tanjore,19th century

३ Bhartrihari, A Reluctant Romantic

Aravinda Rao

At first reading the Shringara Shataka of Bhartrihari seems like an enigma as it not a standard Sanskrit shringara rasa kavya text. In the first section the invocatory verse, 2.1 of the Shataka says that even the three gods, Brahma, Vishnu and Shiva are ensnared by the charms of the god of love and are the slaves of women. In the next verse 2.2 the poet tells us that gestures of women such as the smile, side glances, lilting, lisping words are causes of bondage. In 2.3 he says that seductive looks, gentle revealing movements and coyness are at the same time both embellishments and also weapons for women. This sets the tone for what is to follow. he second section talks of shringara which is in accordance with dharma. For instancethe

Kama and Rati, Rajasthan, 18th century

verse, 2.24 describes the pure love of the married couple. The woman is shy to start with but she sheds her shyness and becomes an active participant in the love sport.

The third section of the Shataka condemns the lustful nature of men and women. The poet is particularly critical of the institution of courtesans, which was socially accepted and prevalent in those times. In 2.58 he warns people to avoid such lustful relationships with such immoral women. Such women are like blazing fires into which lustful men offer their youth and money as oblations. Their outwardly lovely lips are like the spittoons into which several people, spies, cops, thieves, pimps and actors have spat.

Subsequent verses come out strongly against the seductive nature of women and the doting and philandering nature of men. Verse 2.41 says that even learned men are deluded and run after women, praising their doe-eyed beauty, heavy hips, well-formed bosom and lotus face. In 2.53 he warns "Oh mind, the traveler! Do not tread in the dense jungle of the women's body, between the mountains called breasts. There lies a robber named Manmatha." In 2.80 he again wonders how sages such as Vishwamitra and Parasara, forest-dwellers, practicing austerities, surviving on air, water and leaves, were themselves deluded by the charms of lotus faced women. What to talk of all others who eat delicious food along with ghee, milk and curd?

The poet comes out directly in the fourth section of the Shataka, saying that all these attractions will not attract a genuine seeker who controls his mind by the practice of yoga. For such a person, seductive looks, warm embraces of well-formed bosoms and the nectar of lips would look detestable. Just as a jaundiced eye sees things differently when the disease exists, an amorous person gets ensnared by the female charms. Just as a person sees rightly when the disease is cured, in the same way, when the disease of lust ceases in a person, he sees Brahman all-around (2-69).

Is the title Shringara Shataka a misnomer? Or perhaps, the poet has deliberately chosen it to investigate kama and its effect on mankind. Popular stories that the poet was a jilted lover and disillusioned in love, portray an uncharitable picture of him. The world recognises Bhartrihari as a philosopher. What Bhartrihari does is to give us a series of beautiful verses, meant for meditation on the negative aspects of kama and not a celebration of shringara. These can be taken as examples of what Patanjali in his Yoga-Sutras (2-33) calls pratipaksha bhavanam. Bhartrhari's verses could be considered aids for meditation rather than examples of shringara rasa.

Bibliography

Shataka Trayi, (in Telugu) Vavilla Ramaswamy Sastrulu, Chennai. 1926

४ श्रृंगार रस के विलक्षण सर्जक भर्तृहरि और अमरूक

नर्मदा प्रसाद उपाध्याय

मनुश्य रस की निर्मिति है, रस से ही उसकी पहचान बनती है। हमारे शस्त्रकारों ने रस को लेकर गहरा विमर्श किया है किन्तु सहज भाशा में रस वह मानवीय अनुभूति है जो मनुश्य की सर्जनात्मक सामर्थ्य में व्यक्त होती है। मनुश्य की यह रसात्मक सर्जना शिल्प से लेकर शब्द तक में भारतीय इतिहास में प्रत्येक पृश्ठ पर अंकित है फिर यह सर्जना सांची, कोणार्क और खजुराहो के लोचदार पाशाणी शिल्प के रूप में हो या भर्तृहरि, अमरूक और जयदेव के उस शब्द सौश्ठव में जिसमें श्रृंगार की रसमय धाराएं प्रवहमान हैं।

श्रृंगार की इस रसधार को निसृत करने वाले संस्कृत के महान कवियों में हमारे संस्कृत वांग्मय की शतक परम्परा के सर्वाधिक दीप्तिमान नक्षत्र भर्तृहरि हैं जिन्होंने नीतिशतक, श्रृंगारशतक और वैराग्यशतक जैसे काव्य लिखे।

शतक रचयिता भर्तृहरि के अलावा वाक्यपदीय के प्रणेता एक और भर्तृहरि हैं किन्तु अब यह सुनिष्चित हो चुका है कि वाक्यपदीय के रचनाकार तथा श्रृंगारशतक के रचयिता भर्तृहरि भिन्न–भिन्न व्यक्तित्व हैं तथा श्रृंगारशतक के प्रणेता भर्तृहरि, राजा विक्रमादित्य के अग्रज तथा गुरु गोरखनाथ के वह शिश्य थे जिनका समय पांचवीं सदी ईसा पूर्व का था।

हमारे वांग्मय की परम्परा में प्रमुखतः चार प्रकार के शतक सृजित हुए। भक्तिभावपूर्ण, श्रृंगारिक, नीति तथा राष्ट्रीयता से ओतप्रोत। इनमें भक्तिभावपूर्ण अथवा स्रोतात्मक शतक काव्य बहुतायत से रचे गए। इनमें ध्वन्यालोक के रचयिता आनंदवर्धन का देवी शतक, बाणभट्ट का चंडी शतक, मयूर का सूर्य शतक, रंगनाथ ताताचार्य का हनुमत्प्रसाद शतकम्, तिरुवेंकट तात्देशिक का नृसिंह शतक, सुंदराचार्य का कोलम्बाकुच शतक, बल्लथोल नारायण मेनन का कृश्ण शतक तथा विट्ठलदेव मुनि सुंदर शर्मा का श्रीनिवास शतकम् महत्वपूर्ण हैं।

श्रृंगारिक शतकों में भर्तृहरि का श्रृंगार शतक, अमरूक का अमरूक शतक तथा एक अज्ञात कवि का श्रृंगार तिलक शतक शीर्शक प्रमुख हैं। नीतिपरक शतकों में भर्तृहरि का नीति शतक, भल्लर का भल्लर शतक तथा आर.बी. कृष्णमाचारीयर का सुभाशित शतकम् प्रमुख हैं। राष्ट्रीय भावना से ओत प्रोत शतकों में श्री महादेव भारती का भारत शतकम्, डॉ. श्रीधर भास्कर वर्णिकर का मातृभूमि लहरी, उन्हीं का स्वातंत्र वीर शतकम् तथा डॉ. रमाकांत शुक्ल का जय भारत भूमे प्रमुख हैं। गांधी, जवाहरलाल नेहरू तथा इन्दिरा गांधी को लेकर भी शतक रचे गए। इनमें ब्रह्मानंद शुक्ल का गांधी चरितम्, डॉ. रमेशचन्द्र शुक्ल का गांधी गौरवम्, श्रीधर भास्कर वर्णिकर का जवाहर तरंगिणी, कृष्ण सेमवाल का इन्दिरा कीर्ति शतकम् तथा रामकृपालु शास्त्री का इन्दिरा शतक प्रमुख हैं।

इनमें श्रृंगारिक शतक लोकप्रिय भी हैं और साहित्यिक दृश्टि से महत्वपूर्ण भी। भर्तृहरि की वह कथा भी बड़ी लोकप्रिय है जिसमें वे अपनी रानी पिंगला पर गहरे आसक्त थे लेकिन बाद में उसके झूठे प्रणय की जानकारी मिलने पर वे विरागी हो गए। अपनी आसक्ति के समय उन्होंने श्रृंगारशतक लिखा अर्थात् वह श्रृंगारिक काव्य जिसमें शताधिक श्लोक थे और वैराग्य होने पर वैराग्यशतक। भर्तृहरि के श्रृंगार शतक के अंतिम श्लोकों में विराग के स्वर बड़े मुखर हैं जो उनके मोहभंग की सीधी अभिव्यक्ति हैं। उनके श्रृंगार चित्रण की सबसे बड़ी विशेशता है रमणियों के सौन्दर्य के साथ–साथ, पुरुषों को आकृश्ट करने वाले उनके हावभावों का जीवंत चित्रण। उनके पहले ही श्लोक में वे कामदेव की उस सामर्थ्य को स्थापित कर देते हैं जिसके कारण विष्णु और शिव मृग जैसे नेत्रों वाली कामनियों के द्वारा किए जाने वाले गृह कार्यों को स्वयं करने के लिए विवश हैं। वे

हावभाव ऐसे हैं जिसके कारण पुरुष उनके बंधन से छूट नहीं पाता। जैसे मंद–मंद मुस्कुराना, लजाना, भयभीत होना, मुंह फेर लेना, तिरछी नज़र से देखना और तरह–तरह के हावभाव प्रदर्शित करना। श्लोक निम्नानुसार है –

शम्भुस्वयम्भुहरयो हरिणेक्षणानां
येनाक्रियन्त सततं गृहकर्मदासाः।।
वाचामगोचरचरित्रविचित्रिताय
तस्मै नमो भगवते कुसुमायुधाय।। 1।।
स्मितेन भावेन च लज्जया भिया
पराङ्मुखैरर्द्धकटाक्षवीक्षणैः।।
वचोभिरीर्श्याकलहेन लीलया
समस्तभावैः खलु बन्धनं स्त्रियः।। 2।।

फिर ये हावभाव ही अकेले नहीं हैं, इन कामिनियों के आभूशण हैं, चन्द्रमा जैसा मुख, कमल को लज्जित करने वाले नेत्र, सोने की दमक को फीका करने वाली उनकी देह की कांति, भौरों के समूह को पराजित करने वाली केश राशि, गजराज के कर्णस्थल की शोभा को अपमानित करने वाले वक्ष, मनोहर वाणी और कोमलता। भर्तृहरि के इस सूक्ष्म वर्णन से उनकी कामिनियों की कमनीयता को आंकने के कौशल की जानकारी मिल जाती है। श्लोक निम्नानुसार है –

वक्त्रं चन्द्रविडम्बि पङ्कजपरीहासक्षमे लोचने
वर्णः स्वर्णमपाकरिश्णुरलिनीजिश्णुः कचानां चयः।।
वक्षोजाविभकुम्भविभ्रमहरौ गुर्वी नितम्बस्थली
वाचां हारि च मार्दवं युवतिशु स्वाभाविकं मण्डनम्।। 5।।

वे अनेक प्रकार से स्त्रियों के कमनीय गुणों को अपने शब्द सौश्ठव में बांधते हैं। उनके काव्य की ललित शैली में मानो अलंकारों की वर्शा होती है और भावों की सुकुमारता के साथ अनुप्रास, उत्प्रेक्षा और यमक झरने लगते हैं। वे कहते हैं रूप ही जल है, चंचल नेत्र मछलियां हैं, नाभि भंवर है और सिर के बाल सर्प हैं। यह सुंदर तरुणी एक दुस्तर नदी की तरह है जिस नदी में श्रृंगार शास्त्र के प्रवीण सुधिजन स्नान करते हैं। श्लोक निम्नानुसार है –

उन्मीलत्त्रिवलितरङ्गनिलया प्रात्तुङ्गपीनस्तन–
द्वन्द्वेनोद्यतचक्रवाकमिथुना वक्त्राम्बुजोद्भासिनी।।
कान्ताकारधरा नदीयमभितः क्रूराशया नेष्यते
संसारार्णवमज्जनं यदि तदा दूरेण सन्त्यज्यताम्।। 80।।

भर्तृहरि कामिनी की रोमावली को कामदेव द्वारा स्वयं अपने हाथों से लिखी गई सौभाग्य की पंक्ति मानते हैं, उसके नितम्बों की तुलना पर्वतों से करते हैं और इस बात पर विस्मय करते हैं कि उसमें ऐसी असाधारण कुशलता कैसे आ गई कि वह बिना बाण छोड़े केवल अपने गुण से पुरुष के हृदय को बेध देती है। भर्तृहरि के श्रृंगार वर्णन में परिप्रेक्ष्य का अद्भुत विस्तार है। वे कामिनी के यौवन और उसके अंग प्रत्यंगों का वर्णन करते हुए उन्हें अमृत और विश से जोड़ते हैं। वे कहते हैं कि सुंदर नितम्बिनी को छोड़कर न अमृत है, न विष। स्त्री यदि अपने प्रियतम को चाहे तो अमृत लता है और न चाहे तो फिर वह विष की मंजरी है। एक श्लोक में उनकी विलक्षण अभिव्यक्ति है कि स्त्रियों की बातों में अमृत और हृदय में हलाहल होता है इसलिए पुरुष उनके अधरों का पान करते हैं और उनके वक्षों का मर्दन। वे कहते हैं कि स्त्री जब तक आंखों के सामने रहती है तब तक अमृत है और जैसे ही आंखों से दूर होती है तो वह विष से भी अधिक दुखदायी हो जाती है। यहां यह भी विशेश रूप से उल्लेखनीय है कि भर्तृहरि की श्रृंगारिक कविता का आधार पुण्य है। वे कहते हैं कि यदि तुम उसके कठोर स्तनों की प्रभृति का आनंद लेना चाहते हो तो पुण्य करो क्योंकि बिना पुण्य के मनोरथ सिद्ध नहीं होते। श्लोक निम्नानुसार है –

तस्याः स्तनौ यदि घनौ, जघनं च हारि
वक्त्रं च चारु तव चित्त किमाकुलत्वम्।।
पुण्यं कुरुश्व यदि तेशु तवास्ति वाञ्छा
पुण्यैर्विना न हि भवन्ति समीहितार्थाः।। 17।।

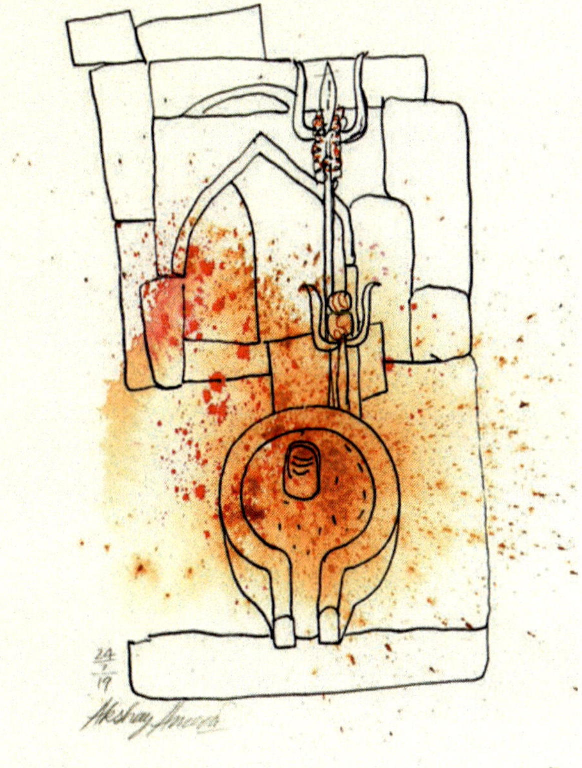

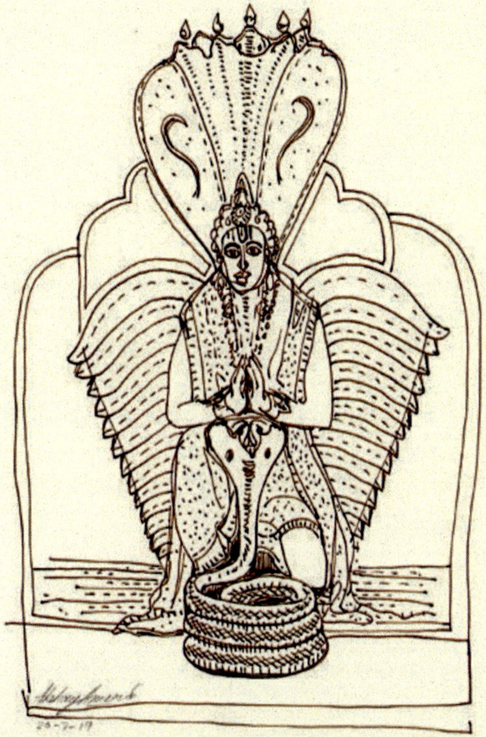

श्रृंगार शतक के 73 श्लोक के बाद भर्तृहरि का वैराग्य जन्म जाता है जिसकी परिणति उनकी इस अभिव्यक्ति में होती है जब वे कहते हैं कि जब तक मुझमें काम का अंधकार था तब तक मुझे सारा संसार स्त्रीमय दिखाई देता था लेकिन अब मैंने आंखों में विवेक का अंजन लगाया है इसलिए मेरी समदृश्टि हो गई है, अब मुझे त्रिलोक की ब्रह्ममय दीखती है। श्लोक निम्नानुसार है –

यदाऽऽसीदज्ञानं स्मरतिमिरसञ्चारजनितं
तदा सर्वं नारीमयमिदमशेशं जगदभूत्।
इदानीमस्माकं पटुतरविवेकाञ्जनदृशां
समीभूता दृश्टिस्त्रिभुवनमपि ब्रहम मनुते।। 101।।

जैसा कि पूर्व में उल्लेख किया गया मनुष्य की अस्मिता रस से रची गई है इसलिए भारतीय वांग्मय की परम्परा रस प्रधान है। संस्कृत काव्य हमारी इस परम्परा की आत्मा है जिसका अंतिम लक्ष्य हृदय में आनंद की प्रतिष्ठा है और इसी आनंद की सृश्टि करने के उद्देश्य से संस्कृत में गीतिकाव्य रचे गए। ये गीतिकाव्य मुक्तक के रूप में भी लिखे गए और प्रबंध के रूप में भी। इनमें भर्तृहरि का श्रृंगार शतक और अमरूक का अमरूक शतक मुक्तक काव्य हैं जबकि कालिदास का मेघदूत प्रबंध काव्य है। उसे संदेश काव्य भी कहते हैं।

भर्तृहरि के बाद सातवीं सदी में अमरूक हुए जिनके काव्य की भूरि–भूरि प्रशंसा करते हुए आनंदवर्धन ने कहा कि अमरूक के मुक्तक रस से इतने भरे हुए हैं कि वे प्रबंध काव्य की क्षमता रखते हैं। श्लोक निम्नानुसार है –

मुक्तकेषु हि प्रबन्धेश्विव रसावबन्धामिवोहीनः कवयो दृश्यन्ते।
अमरूकश्य कवे मुक्तका श्रृंगारस्यन्दिनः प्रबन्धायमाणाः प्रसिद्धा एव

अमरूक प्रेम के, श्रृंगार के अद्भुत आख्याता हैं। उनका श्रृंगार वर्णन भाव और भंगिमा दोनों को साधता है लेकिन उनका काव्य जैसा कि अमरूक शतक के पाश्चात्य समीक्षक एन्ड्रयू शीलिंग कहते हैं, विरह की ओर अधिक उन्मुख है। अमरूक की नायिका अपने विरह को बांट देती है और केवल प्राण अपने पास रखती है। वहां आंसुओं को अपनी सखियों को, चिंता गुरुजनों को, दैन्य परिजनों को और सहेलियां उसके पीछे लगी हैं उन्हें अपना मन और ताप सौंप देती है क्योंकि उसे लगता है कि वह जल्दी ही प्राणों से मुक्त हो जाएगी।

एक अल्प वय वाली नायिका के पति जब कहीं जाने को तत्पर होते हैं तो वह उन्हें दूसरे ढंग से रोकती है। वह न तो नायक के वस्त्र का छोर थामती है, न दरवाज़ा बंद करती है, न पैर पड़कर रुकने का आग्रह करती है लेकिन अंधियारी रात में जब नायक जाने को तत्पर होता है तो वह अपनी आंखों से आंसुओं की बरसात कर देती है। श्लोक निम्नानुसार है –

लग्ना नांशुकपल्लवे भुजलता न द्वारदेशेऽर्पिता
नो वा पाद्युगे स्वयं निपतितं तिश्ठेति नोक्तं वचः।
काले केवलमम्बुदालिमलिने गन्तुं प्रवृत्तः षठ–
स्तन्व्या बाश्पजलौघकल्पितनदीपूरेण रुद्धः प्रियः ।। 62।।

अमरूक की एक नायिका ऐसी है जिसे उसकी सखी समझाती है कि वह थोड़ा तो मान करे, अपनी सिधाई कम करे तब वह नायिका अपनी सखी से कहती है कि ज़रा धीरे बोलो क्योंकि उसके प्राणेष्वर उसके हृदय में ही तो बैठे हैं। अमरूक की एक नायिका ऐसी है जो रात भर नायक के साथ रस चर्चा करती रही, उनका तोता भी उनके साथ ही था। जब सुबह हुई तो गुरुजनों के सामने तोते ने उस रसचर्चा को ऊंची आवाज़ में दोहराना षुरु किया तब लज्जा के कारण नायिका ने अपने कान में लटक रहे लाल के टुकड़े को अनार के दाने के बहाने तोते के मुंह में डाल दिया ताकि उसका मुंह बंद हो जाए।

अमरूक की नायिका की भंगिमाओं की अद्भुत पराकाष्ठा उस ष्लोक में है जिसमें अचानक प्रिय के आने का समाचार सुनकर उसे यह नहीं सूझता कि वह उसका स्वागत कैसे करे ? तब वह अपने अंगों से ही मंगल रचती है। अमरूक कहते हैं कि उसने नीलकमल, कुंद और मालती के फूलों से नहीं बल्कि अपनी दृश्टि की डोर से ही बंदनवार बनाया और मंगल कलशों से नहीं बल्कि पसीने में भीगे अपने कुच कलशों से अपने प्रिय को अर्घ्य दिया। श्लोक निम्नानुसार है –

'दीर्घा वन्दनमालिका विरचिता दृश्ट्यैव नेन्दीवरैः
पुश्पाणां प्रकरः स्मितेन रचितो नो कुन्दजात्यादिभिः।
दत्तः स्वेदमुचा पयोधरभरेणार्घो न कुम्भाम्भसा
स्वैरेवावयवैः प्रियस्य विषतस्तन्व्या कृतं मंङ्गलम्ः।। 45।।

और यही स्थिति अमरूक के नायक की है। जब जल के भार से अलसाए बादल गरजे तब उद्विग्न होकर, आंखों में आंसू भरकर उसने इतनी विव्हलता के साथ विरह का गीत गाया कि संवेदनशील लोगों ने इस भय से अपने कान तुरंत मूंद लिए कि कहीं उनके हृदय टूट न जाएं। अमरूक के नायक की दशा बड़ी विचित्र है जो उसके मित्र के साथ उसके द्वारा किए जा रहे संवाद में प्रगट होती है। नायक का नया–नया प्रेम हुआ है, वह अपने मित्र से कहता है कि बड़ी विचित्र बात है कि दोष नहीं है लेकिन उसके कारण विकलता कहीं और है। नायिका तो वह है परंतु उसे पाने के लिए बावला मैं हो रहा हूं। स्त्री वह है लेकिन कातरता मुझमें है। स्तन उसके बड़े–बड़े हैं लेकिन बोझिल मैं हूं और विशाल नितम्ब उसके हैं लेकिन गति मेरी अवरुद्ध है। श्लोक निम्नानुसार है –

रात्रौ वारिभरालसाम्बुदरवोद्विग्नेन जाताश्रणा
पान्थेनात्मवियोगदुःखपिशनुं गीतं तथोत्कण्ठया।
आस्तां जीवितहारिणः प्रवसनालापस्य संकीर्तनं
मानस्थापि जलाञ्जलिः सरभसं लोकेन दत्तो यथा।। 54।।

इस तरह अमरूक शतक के नायक और नायिका प्रेम के उस अथाह सागर में डूबे हुए हैं जिसकी तरंगों में इतनी सामर्थ्य नहीं कि वे उन्हें अतल से उबारकर तट पर छोड़ दें। जैसा कि पूर्व में उल्लेख किया गया है श्रृंगार शतक तथा अमरूकशतक मुक्तक काव्य हैं। संस्कृत काव्य में ग्यारहवीं सदी से अठारहवीं सदी के बीच मुक्त काव्य की परम्परा में अनेक नई विधाएं समाविष्ट हुईं तथा इसी अवधि में मुक्तक के श्रेष्ठ कवियों का आविर्भाव हुआ जिन्होंने बड़ी संख्या में भक्तिपरक स्त्रोत काव्य लिखे। इस काल में संदेष काव्य, शतक, अष्टक, खण्ड काव्य तथा संघात जैसी विधाओं में भी अनेक रचनाएं की गईं।

भर्तृहरि का श्रृंगारशतक अद्‌भुत है। इसमें स्त्रियों के गुणों के समक्ष वे नतमस्तक हैं। प्रख्यात संस्कृत विद्वान डॉ. राधावल्लभ त्रिपाठी के अनुसार श्रृंगारशतक में स्त्री प्रशंसा, संभोग वर्णन, कामिनीगर्हणा, सुविरक्तदुर्विरक्तपद्धति तथा ऋतु वर्णन जैसे विशय हैं। श्रृंगारशतक में भर्तृहरि ने श्रृंगार का चटकपूर्ण वर्णन किया है। स्त्री हृदय के भावों को परख कर उन्होंने अपने काव्य में बांधा है तथा प्रेम से प्रभावित कामी व्यक्तियों के चित्त में जो वृत्तियां विद्यमान रहती हैं उनका सूक्ष्म अवलोकन करते हुए उन्होंने इस विषय को तथा इससे जुड़े हुए परिणामों को व्यक्त किया है। लेकिन यह

समूचे श्रृंगारिक संस्कृत काव्य की विशेशता है कि उसकी अभिव्यक्ति में तप की अंतर्धारा प्रवाहित होती है तथा यह तथ्य भर्तृहरि के श्रृंगारशतक तथा अमरूक के अमरूकशतक से लेकर जयदेव के गीतगोविन्द तक विद्यमान है। उन्होंने श्रृंगारशतक के अंतिम श्लोकों में वैराग्य के प्रति अपना स्पश्ट झुकाव दर्शाया है। वे पुण्य के बिना श्रृंगार के उपभोग को नहीं मान्य करते।

वे उन पुरुशों को धन्य मानते हैं जो चंचल और बड़ी–बड़ी आंखों वाली यौवन के अभिमान से पूर्ण, दृढ़ और पुष्ट स्तनों वाली तथा क्षीण उदरभाग पर त्रिवली से सुशोभित स्त्रियों की सूरत देखकर मन में किसी प्रकार का विकार नहीं लाते। श्लोक निम्नानुसार है –

धन्यास्त एव तरलायतलोचनानां
तारुण्यदर्पघनपीनपयोधराणाम्।।
क्षामोदरोपरिलसत्त्रिवलीलतानां
दृश्ट्वाऽऽकृतिं विकृतिमेति मनो न यषाम्।। 92।।

इसे कवि ने अपने शब्दों में आधुनिक समय में कुछ इस तरह बांधा है।

क्षीण लङ्क अरु पीन कुच, लखि तिय के दृग तीर।
जे अधीर नहिं करत मन, धन्य धन्य ते धीर।।

श्रृंगारशतक के अंतिम श्लोक तक आते–आते भर्तृहरि का वैराग्य पूर्णतः जागृत हो जाता है और जैसा कि पूर्व में उल्लेख किया गया है उनकी आंखों में समाया काम का अंधकार छट जाता है। जबकि अमरूक की सृजन यात्रा में वैराग्य उनकी नियति नहीं है। उनका झुकाव विरह की ओर है। जबकि भर्तृहरि के काव्य में विरह का स्वर प्रमुख नहीं है। भर्तृहरि के काव्य में यद्यपि नायिका के हावभावों की छटा विद्यमान है किन्तु अमरूक का तो पूरा काव्य ही भंगिमा प्रधान काव्य है तथा उसके मूल में नायिका का आंतरिक सौन्दर्य विद्यमान है। अपने पति के परदेश जाने पर अनुभव होने वाली भाव विव्हलता और उसके आने का समाचार सुनने पर सभी अंग प्रत्यंगों के हर्श से भर जाने का भावपूर्ण वर्णन अमरूक के काव्य में है।

अमरूक की कविता में हाल की गाथा सप्तशती की भांति वर्शाकाल के अधिक चित्र हैं। उसमें वसंत के चित्र भी हैं लेकिन वे अपेक्षाकृत कम हैं। भर्तृहरि ने हेमन्त, शिशिर व ग्रीश्म ऋतुओं को भी अपनी कविता में बांधा है। इस तरह वे प्रकृति की छटा को अपनी शब्द छटा में अभिव्यक्त करते

हैं। जबकि अमरूक का केन्द्रीय भाव नायक और नायिका के बीच संवाद और क्रियाओं का रहता है। अमरूक के काव्य का आधार उज्जवल श्रृंगार है। उनके काव्य की एक और विशेशता यह है कि उसमें सहजता है। अलंकरणों से सज्जित करने का यत्नपूर्वक प्रयास उन्होंने नहीं किया है बल्कि उनका प्रयास यह है कि शब्द अर्थ प्रधान हों और उनके संप्रेषण की सामर्थ्य अधिक हो। वे उस प्रेम को अपनी कविता में बांधते हैं जो तरह–तरह की भंगिमाओं में ढलकर अपने प्रिय को समर्पित हो जाता है। उनकी कविता व्यंजक है। उसमें न तो भावों की पुनरावृत्ति है न आवेग की अतिरंजना। अमरूक प्रेम के अप्रतिम आख्याता हैं। उनके काव्य में छलकने वाला प्रेम ऐसा शुद्ध और निष्छल प्रेम है जिसका पर्याय केवल प्रेम ही है।

इस तरह भर्तृहरि और अमरूक के शतकों में विद्यमान श्रृंगार रस के संबंध में यह निश्कर्श निकाला जा सकता है कि इन दोनों ही अप्रतिम कवियों ने माधुर्य से परिपूर्ण रूप के रसपूर्ण बिम्ब रचे हैं। भर्तृहरि और अमरूक की बिम्ब रचना में भंगिमाओं का अंतर है। अमरूक की रचना में भाव विव्हलता की पराकाष्ठा है जबकि भर्तृहरि भंगिमाओं के माध्यम से रस का उद्रेक करते हैं।

इन महान कवियों के द्वारा रचे गए बिम्ब ऐसे हैं जिनमें रूप की ऐसी रस माधुरी छलकती है जिसका प्रवह कभी विराम नहीं पाता इसलिए कि प्रेम की अस्मिता कालबंधनों से परे होती है और प्रेम के रूप में उसके प्राण अमर हुआ करते हैं।

29.12
2019

Kama on a composite elephant, Painting by Vijay Sharma

1.

Salutations to Madana, the god of love, whose banner is the fish,
whose weapon is the flower,
who enslaved even the supreme gods Brahma,
Vishnu and Mahesh to doe eyed women,
and whose tricks are difficult to describe with words.

2.

Lotus faced young women with dancing eyes,
who by the movement of their brows,
at other times by looking down bashfully or
pretending to be afraid or by being playful,
as if fill all the directions with the (fragrance of) fully blossomed blue lotuses.

3.

O! innocent woman with sideling glances and playful langour
whence did you acquire the art of archery
because of which you could pierce the heart of men even without an arrow?

- भर्तृहरि - वसंततिलका

शम्भुः स्वयम्भुहरयो हरिणेक्षणानां
येनाक्रियन्त सततं गृहकर्मदासाः ॥
वाचामगोचरचरित्रविचिविताय
तस्मै नमो भगवते कुसुमायुधाय ॥१॥

- भर्तृहरि - शिखरिणी

क्वचित्सभ्रूभङ्गैः क्वचिदपि च लज्जापरिणतैः
क्वचिभ्दीतित्रस्तैः क्वचिदपि च लीलाविलसतैः ॥
नवोढानामेतैर्वदनकमलैर्नेत्रलितैः स्फुरैत्नी -
लाब्जानां प्रकरपरिपूर्वा इवै दिशः ॥२॥

- भर्तृहरि - अनुष्टुभ्

मुग्धे! धानुष्कता केयमपूर्वा त्वति दृश्यते ।
यया विध्यसि चेतांसि गुणैरेव न सायकैः ॥३॥

4.

Fortunate is the man who will be able to have pleasure with a sinless
and beautiful woman bestowed to him by Brahma,
who is like a flower which no one has smelt,
like a fleshy and fresh leaf untouched by nails,
like a pearl which has not been perforated,
like honey which has not yet been tasted.

5.

A gentle smile on her face, a sincere look in her eyes,
her voice resonating with amorous sounds,
her gait like the flutter of new leaves on a creeper, graceful as a young bud
whose doe eyes are on the verge of moving from innocence to maturity,
everything about her is attractive.

6.

Let me be bitten by a long hungry blue coloured snake with a winding gait
but not by a woman who has a serpentine sarcastic glance.
There are many honorable physicians who can cure snake bites
but there is no mantra or medicine for someone who has been struck by a woman's glance.

- भर्तृहरि - शिखरिणी

अनाघ्रातं पुष्पं; किसलयमलूनं कररुहैं----
रनाविद्धं रत्नं मधु नवमनास्वादितरसम् ।।
अखण्डं पुण्यानां फलमिव च तद्रूपमनघं
ना जाणे भोक्तारं कमिह समुपस्थास्यति विधिः ।।४।।

- भर्तृहरि - शिखरिणी

स्मितं किञ्चिद् वक्त्रे सरलतरलो दृष्टिविभवः
परिस्पन्दो वाचामभिनवविलासोक्तिसरसः ।।
मतानामारम्भः किसलयितलीलापरिकरः
स्पृशन्त्यास्तारूण्यं किमिह न हि रम्यं मृगदृशः ।।५।।

- भर्तृहरि - शार्दूलविक्रिडित

व्यादीर्घेण चलेन वक्रगतिना तेजस्विनी भोगिना
नीलाब्जद्युतिनाऽहिना वरमहो दष्टो न तच्चक्षुषा ।
्दष्टे सन्ति चिकित्सा दिशि दिशि प्रायेण धर्मौर्थिनो
मुग्धाक्षीक्षणवीक्षितस्य नहि मे मन्त्रो न चाप्यौषम् ।।६।।

7.

With a gentle smile, expressing her feelings, bashfully feigning fear,
turning and casting a side long glance, mimicking playfulness and anger,
with all these a woman binds a man.

8.

Cleverly moving her eye brows, with a half closed side long glance,
sweet conversation, smiling bashfully, playfully walking and standing,
these are the adornments as well weapons of a woman.

9.

A face that puts the moon to shame, eyes that rival the lotus,
colour that exceeds that of gold, the colour of her hair better than that of wasps,
her voluptuous breasts swaying like an elephant,
full buttocks and sweet speech. These are her natural endowments.

भर्तृहरि- वंशस्थ

स्मितेन भावेन च लज्जया भिया
पराङ्मुखैरर्धकटाक्षवीक्षणैः ॥
वचोभिरीर्ष्या कलहेन लीलया
समस्तभावैः खलु बन्धनं स्त्रियः ॥७॥

भर्तृहरि- शालिनी

भ्रूचातुर्याकुञ्चिताक्षाः कटाक्षाः
स्निग्धा वाचो लज्जिताश्चैव हासाः ॥
लीलामन्दं प्रस्थितं च स्थितं च
स्त्रीणामेतद् भूषणं चायुधं च ॥८॥

भर्तृहरि- शार्दूलविक्रीडित

वक्त्रं चन्द्रविडम्बि पङ्कजपरीहासक्षमे लोचने
वर्णः स्वर्णमपाकरिष्णुरलिनीजिष्णुः कचानां चयः ॥
वक्षोजाविभकुम्भविभ्रमहरौ मुर्वी नितम्बस्थली
वाचां हारि च मार्दवं युवतिपु स्वाभाविकं मण्डनम् ॥९॥

10.

What are best of objects that are beautiful to behold? A face with does eyes radiant with love.
What is the most alluring fragrance? The aroma of the mouth of a young woman.
What is the best sound? The speech of a woman.
What is the sweetest taste? The taste of the lips of a beautiful woman.
What is the most pleasurable touch? The soft body of a young woman.
What is that which a romantic person longs for? The amorous play of a young woman.

11.

A woman whose waist ornament has a tinkling sound when she moves,
and whose anklets makes a sonorous sound, whose gait removes the pride of the royal swan,
that frightened doe eyed woman with piercing glances, whose heart will she not steal?

12.

What woman does not capture a man, on whose body there is a saffron coloured unguent,
on whose breasts a necklace that sways, on whose lotus feet the swans on her anklets sing?

13.

A woman whose star lit and flickering glances win over Indra,
why do poets call these sensuous woman as weak?
I think they are foolish.

भर्तृहरि-   शार्दूलविक्रीडित
द्रष्टव्येषु किमुत्तमं मृगदृशां प्रेमाप्रसन्नं मुखं घ्रात-
व्येष्वपि किं तदास्यपवनः श्राव्येषु किं तद्व चः ॥
किं स्वाद्येषु तदोष्ठपल्लवरसः स्पृश्येषु किं तत्तनुर्ध्येयं
किं नवयौवनं सुहृदयैः सर्वत्र तद्विभ्रमः ॥१०॥

भर्तृस्ज्;हरि- वसंततिलका १३३
एताश्चलद्वलयसंहतिमेखलोत्थ-
झंकारनू पुरपराजितराजहंस्यः ॥
कुर्वस्ज्;न्ति कस्य न मनो विवशं तरुण्यो
वित्रस्तमुग्धहसिदृशैः कटाक्षैः ॥११॥

भर्तृहरि- दोधक
कुङ् कुमपपङ्क्कलङ्कितदेहा गौरपयोधरकम्पितहारा ।
नूपुरहंसरणत्पदपद्माके न वशीकुरुते भुवि रामा? ॥१२॥

भर्तृहरि- वसंततिलका
नूनं हि ते कविवरा विपरीतबोधा
ये नित्यमाहुरबला इति कामिनीस्ताः ॥
वाभिर्विलोलतरतारकदृष्टिपातैः
शकादयोऽपि विजितास्त्वलाः कथं ताः? ॥१३॥

14.

The glance of a woman is like a sharp needle, which captured even Indra,
which pierces your mind and with it she able to send
Kamadev with a silken thread as a messenger.

15.

You are born with lovely white teeth. Your breast are adorned with a pearl necklace.
Your hair tied carefully
Even though your body appears pure and peaceful
why is it that we are so disturbed sensuously?

16.

Around me there are lamps, the flames of fire and many gems.
However without my doe eyed beloved all this is filled with darkness.

17.

O! Beautiful woman, your uplifted breasts, restless eyes, dancing eyebrows,
your lips coloured red either naturally or because you are angry.
Let all these be, for it seems as if they are lines written by Madana
as if it were a garland of auspicious syllables
Even if these be true or false, yet why does it excites me?

भर्तृहरि- अनुष्टभ्

नूनमाज्ञाकरस्तस्याः सुभ्रुवो मकरध्वजः ।
यतस्तन्नेत्रसञ्चारसूचितेषु प्रवर्तते ॥१४॥

भर्तृहरि- शार्दूलविक्रीडित

केशाः संयमिनः श्रुतेरपि परं पारं गते लोचने
अन्तर्वक्त्रमपि स्वभावशुचिभिः कीर्णं द्विजानां गणैः ॥
मुक्तानां सतताधिवासरुचिरौ वक्षोजकुम्भाविमा-
वित्थं तन्वि! वपुः प्रशान्तमपि ते क्षोभं करोत्येव नः ॥१५॥

भर्तृहरि - अनुष्टभ

सति प्रदीपे सत्यग्नौ नानामणिष्वपि ।
विना मे मृगशावाक्ष्या तमोभूतमिदं जगत् ॥१६॥

भर्तृहरि- शार्दूलविक्रीडित

उद्वृत्तः स्तनभार एष तरले नेत्रे चले भ्रूलते
रागाधिष्ठितमोष्ठपल्लवमिदं कुर्वन्तु नाम व्यथाम् ॥
सौभाग्याक्षरमालिकेव लिखिता पुष्पायुधेन स्वयं
मध्यस्थाऽपि करोति तापमधिकं रोमावली केन सा? ॥१७॥

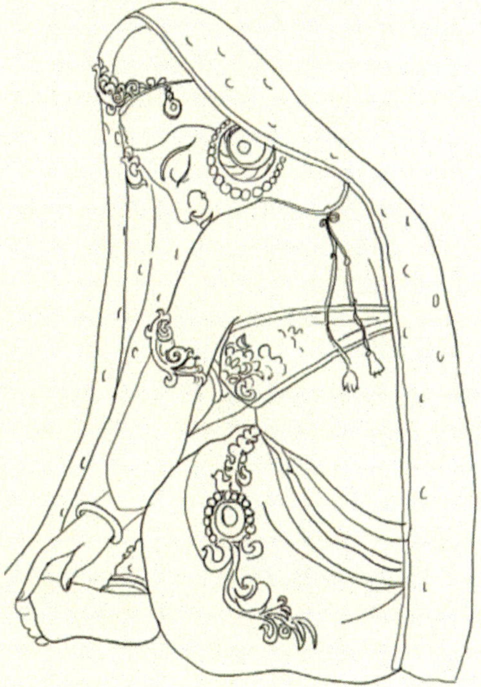

18.

The face of a beautiful woman is like the *chandrakanta* gem.
Blue black tresses are like the *mahaneel* gem.
The palms are red like the lotus or the *padmarag* gem.
The bejewelled woman is truly beautiful.

19.

A woman is like the planets, her radiant face is like the Moon,
her breasts are like Jupiter and her feet are like Saturn.

20.

Why are you attracted towards (a woman with) voluptuous breasts,
beautiful face and wide buttocks?
If you want to possess this (woman) you need to be morally righteous,
without this your wish will not be granted.

21.

Women attract men, intoxicate them, make a fool of them, censure them
and play with them and make their mind sad and restless.
Detecting a soft heart what is it that they will not do?

- भार्तृहरि - अनुष्टुभ्
मुखेन चन्द्रकान्तेन महानीलैः शिरोरुहैः ।।
पाणिभ्यां पद्मरागाभ्यां रेजे रत्नमयीव सा ।।१८।।

- भार्तृहरि - अनुष्टुभ
गुरुणा स्तनभारेण मुखचन्द्रेण भास्वता ।।
शनैश्चराभ्यां पादाभ्यां रेजे ग्रहमयीव सा ।।१९।।

भर्तृस्ज्;हरि- वसंततिलका १४०
यस्याः स्तनौ यदि घनौ जघनं विहारि
वक्त्रं च चारु तव चित्त किमालुकत्वम् ।।
पुण्यं कुरुत्;व यदि र्तेत्;ु तवास्ति वाञ्छा
पुण्यैर्विस्ज्;ना नहि भवन्ति समीहितार्थास्ज्;ः ।।२०।।

भर्तृहरि- वसंततिलका
संमोहयन्ति मदयन्ति विडम्बयन्ति
निर्भर्त्सयन्ति यन्ति रमयन्ति विषादयन्तिः ।।
एताः प्रविश्य हृदयं सदयं नराणां किं नाम
वामनयना न समाचरन्ति ।।२१।।

22.

An accomplished man will have the light of discrimination shine
in his mind as long as a doe eyed woman
does not assault him with piercing glances.

23.

Pandits who boast of their Vedantic prowess
and talk about sensual detachment are silenced by the sound of the tinkling
of women's waist ornament adorned with red jewels.

24.

Pretentious pandits who malign young women,
delude others and themselves
because the fruit of penance is heaven,
where they get *apsaras*.

25.

With their dancing serpentine eyebrows,
women play with men with uncontrolled senses
and succeed in destroying their concentration (samadhi)
and create sensual desires in their mind.

भर्तृस्ज;हरि- रथोद्धता
तावदेव कृतिनां हृदि
स्फुरत्र्येट्;ा निर्मस्ज;लविवेकदीपकः ।।
यावदेवं न कुरङ्गचक्षुट्;ां
ताड्यते चपललोचनाञ्चलैः ।।२२।।

भर्तृस्ज;हरि- मालिनी
वचसि भवति सङ्गत्यागमुद्दिश्य वार्तास्ज;
श्रुतिमुखमुखराणां केवलं पण्डितानाम् ।।
जघनमरुणरत्नंग्रन्थिकाञ्चीकलापं
कुवलयनयनानां को विहातुं समर्थस्ज;ः? ।।२३।।

भर्तृस्ज;हरि- आर्यास्ज;
स्वपरप्रतारकोऽसौ निन्दति
योऽलीकपण्डितो युवतीः ।।
यस्मात्तपसोऽपि फलं स्वर्गस्ज;ः
स्वर्गेऽपि चाप्सरसः ।।२४।।

भर्तृहरि- अनुष्टभ्
अजितात्मसु संबध्दः समाधिकृतचापलः ।।
भुजञ्जकुटिलः स्तब्धो भ्रूविक्षेपः खलायते ।।२५।।

26.

A man can walk on the righteous path, control his senses,
be modest and morally upright
Until his heart is pierced by the sharp arrows of women's glances
discharged from their arched eyebrows and blue eyelashes.

27.

When learned saints like Visvamitra and Parashar who lived on leaves of trees and water
were thrown into a state of intoxication at the sight of lotus faced women
How is possible for those who eat rice, wheat, milk and ghee to keep control of their senses?
To contorl lust is wordly men is as impossible as the crossing of the Vindhya over the sea.

28.

She is herself the embodiment of nectar and
the cause of arousing passionate love in the hearts of people.
Men who want a cure for their debilitating illness
drink the ambrosia of your lips with the pearl that hangs from your nose.

29.

This world is full of sorrow and the root cause of misery.
Thus we may criticize the world but it is difficult to conquer it.
The mind of even the wise can burn in the fires of Kama.

भर्तृहरि- स्त्रीग्धर

सन्मार्गे तावदास्ते प्रभवति पुरुषस्तावदेवेन्द्रियाणां
लज्जां तावद्विधत्ते विनयमपि समालंबले तावदेव ॥
भ्रूचापाकृष्टामुक्ताः श्रवणपथगता नीलपक्ष्माण एते
यावल्लीलावतीनां हृदि न धृतिमुषो दृष्टिबाणाः पतन्ति ॥२६॥

भर्तृहरि- शार्दूलविक्रीडित

विश्वामित्रपराशरप्रभृतयो वाताम्बुपर्णाशनास्तेऽपि
स्त्रीमुखपङ्कजं सुललितं दृष्टैव मोहं गताः ॥
शाल्यन्नं सघृतं पयोदधियुतं भुञ्जन्ति ये मानवा-
स्तेषामिन्द्रियनिग्रहो यदि भवेद्विन्ध्यस्तरेत्सागरम् ॥२७॥

भर्तृहरि- उपजाति

सुधामयोऽपि क्षयरोगशान्त्यै नासाग्रमुक्ताफलकच्छलेन ॥
अनङ्गसञ्जीवनदृष्टिशक्तिर्मुखामृतं ते पिबवीत चन्द्रः ॥२८॥

भर्तृहरि- शिखरिणा

असाराः सन्त्वेते विरतिविरसायासविषया
जुगुप्सन्तां यद्वा ननु सकलोदोषास्पदमिति ॥
तथाऽप्यन्तस्तत्त्वे प्रणिहितधियामप्यतिबलस्त-
दीयोऽनाख्येयः स्फुरति हृदये कोऽपि महिमा ॥२९॥

30

Kamadev in the form of a spider spreads its net in the form of a woman in this wide samsara.
Using her lips as a bait Kamadev draws fish (men) into the net and cooks them in the fire of love.

31.

A woman's body is like a forest and her breasts are like hard to reach mountains.
O mind! Do not roam there because Kamadev like a thief hides there.

32.

The terrible convulsions created by Kamadev do not respond to mantras,
they cannot be cured by medicines,
they cannot be destroyed by hundreds of peace giving cures.
In that condition he is given to delusions and strong fits and his vision is distorted.

33.

How long can nobility, learning, pride in one's ancestry and thoughtfulness last?
Only as long as Kamadev has not afflicted your body with his fire.

भर्तृहरि- वसंततिलका
विस्तारितं मकरकेतनधीवरेण
स्त्रीसंज्ञितं बडिशमत्र भवाम्बुराशौ ।।
तेनाचिरात्तदधरामिषलोलमर्त्य-
मत्स्यान्विकृष्य स पचत्यनुरागवह्नौ ।।३०।।

- भार्तृहरि - अनुष्टभ्
कामिनीकायकान्तारे स्तनपर्वतदुर्गमे ।
मा सञ्चर मनःपान्थ ! तत्रास्ते स्मरतस्करः ।।३१।।

भर्तृहरि- शिखरिणा
न गम्यो मन्त्राणां न च भवति भैषज्यविषयो
न चापि प्रध्वंसं व्रजति विविधैःशान्तिकशतैः ।।
भ्रमावेशादङ्गे कमपि विदधद्भङ्गमसकृत्
स्मरापस्मारोऽयं भ्रमयति दृशं घूर्णयति च ।।३२।।

- भार्तृहरि - अनुष्टुम्
तावन्महत्वं पाण्डित्यं कुलीनत्वं विवेकिता ।
यावज्ज्वलति नाङ्गेषु हन्त पञ्चेपुपावकः ।।३३।।

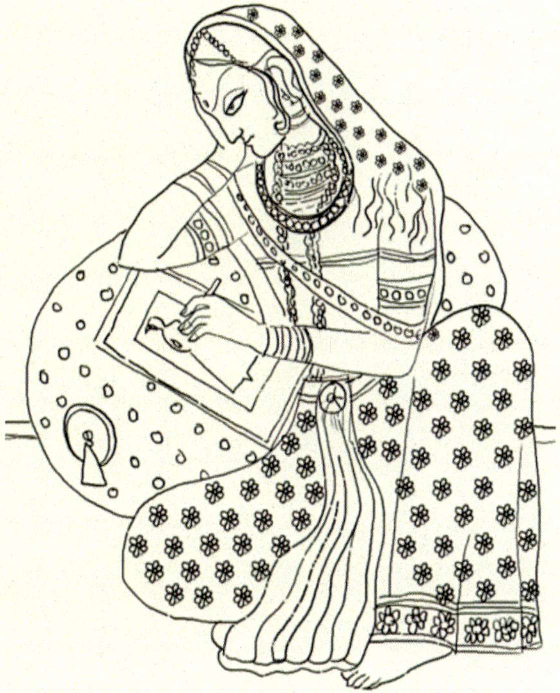

34.

The stamp (command) of Madana is a woman who carries out all his work.
Madana heartlessly attacks a man who rejects (this woman)
and who wanders looking for false fruits.
He disrobes him, shaves his head, gives him five pigtails, covers his hair into knots
or gives him a skull to go and beg (like Shankara).

35.

A dog (man) who is emaciated, squinted, lame, deaf, with a broken tail,
with pus oozing from wounds, covered with worms, hungry, old with a necklace of pots
afflicted by Madana runs after a bitch (woman).
Madana punishes even such a man.

36.

There are men who can control an intoxicated elephant,
there are others who can kill a mighty lion.
But it is worth remembering that such men can rarely defeat the pride of Madana.

भर्तृहरि-   शार्दूलविक्रीडित
स्त्रीमुद्रां झपकेतनस्यं परमां सर्वार्थसम्पकरीं
ये मुढाः प्रविहाय यान्ति कुधियो मिथ्याफलान्वेषिणः ।।
ते तेनैव निहत्य नग्नीकृता मुण्डिताः
केचित्पश्चशिखीकृताश्च जटिलाः कापालिकाश्चापरे ।।३४।।

- भार्तृहरि - शिखरिणा
कृशः काणः खश्चः श्रवणरहितः पुच्छविकलो
व्रणी पूयल्लिन्नः कृमिकुलशतैरावृततनुः ।।
क्षुधाक्षामो जीर्णः पिङ्गरककपालार्पितगलः
शुनीमन्वेति श्वा! हतमपि च हत्व्येव मदनः ।।३५।।

भर्तृहरि- वसंततिलका
मत्तेभकुम्भदलने भुवि सन्ति शूराः
केचित्प्रचण्डमृगराजवधेऽपि दक्षाः ।।
किन्तु ब्रवीमि वलिनां पुरतः प्रसह्य
कंदर्पदर्पदलने विरला मनुष्याः ।।३६।।

37.

Fragrant winds blowing, new leaves sprouting, the *kokila* with her sweet voice of longing
and drops of sweat on the moon like face of a beloved.
On a spring night who does not show their strengths?

38.

In the spring season even when the kokila sings sweetly
and the cool breeze (fragrant with sandalwood) from the Malaya blows
it causes pain to the body and mind to those who long for their beloved.
In times of trouble even nectar seems like poison.

39.

Blessed is he who is in the amorous company of the beloved even though she is feigning anger,
(sitting) in the cool light of the moon,
in a flowering love pavilion listening to the sweet melody of the *kokila,*
in a pleasant conversation with a poet.

वसंत-निदाध-ग्रीष्म, चैत्र.

भर्तृहरि- हरिणा

परिमलभृतो वाताः शाखा नवाङ्कुरकोटयो
मधुरविरूतोत्कण्ङ्गा वाचः प्रियाः पिकपक्षिणाम् ॥
विरलसुरतस्वेदोद्गारा वधूवदनेन्दवः
प्रसरति मधौ रात्र्यां जातो न कस्य गुणोदयः? ॥३७॥

भर्तुहुरि- द्रुतविलंबित

मधूरयं मधुरैरपि कोकिला-
कलरवैर्मलयस्य च वायुभिः ॥
विरहिणः प्रहिणस्ति शरीरिणो
विपदि हन्त सुधाऽपि विषायते ॥३८॥

भर्तृहरि- शार्दूलविक्रीडित

आवासः किलकिञ्चितस्य दयिताः पार्श्वे विलासालसाः
कर्णे कोकिलकामिनीकलरवः स्मेरो लतामण्डपः ॥
गोष्ठी सत्कविभिः समं कतिपयैः सेव्याः सितांशोः कराः
केषांचित्सुखयन्ति धन्यहृदयं चैत्रे विचित्राः क्षपाः ॥३९॥

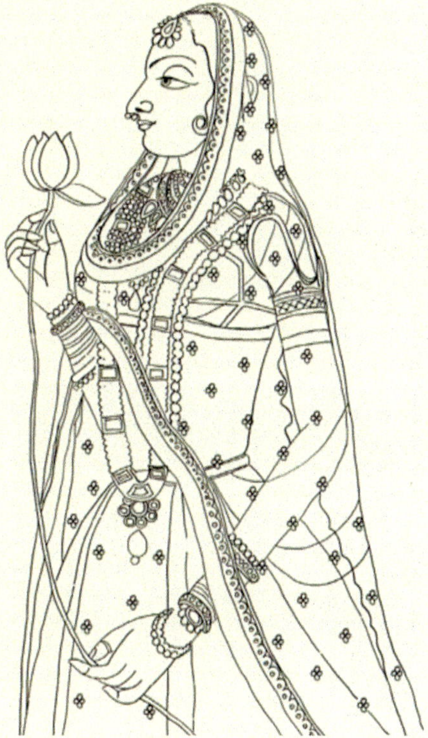

40.

When the kokila longingly looks at the mango blossom
and fresh Malaya winds bring the fragrance of *Palasha* flowers
which assuages the fatigue of the body and mind.
This disturbs even more the beloved who (already) has a fire of longing in her heart.

41.

The beloved's petulance lasts only until
soft Malalay winds with the fragrance of sandalwood blow.

42.

When the intoxicating fragrance of mango blossoms spreads in all directions
and the bees are drunk with honey,
in this season of spring who cannot long for his beloved?

43.

In the summer season when a sensuous woman who has applied sandalwood paste on her arms,
there are flowing fountains, flowers, moonlight, scented soft winds and clear waters.
These invoke desire for sensual pleasures in languid people.

भर्तृहरि- शार्दूलविक्रीडित
पान्थस्त्रीविरहाग्नितीव्रतरतामातन्वती माञ्जरी
माकन्देषु पिकाङ्गनाभिरधुना सोत्कण्ठमालोक्यते ॥
अप्येते नवपाटलीपरिमलप्राग्भारपाटच्चरा
वान्ति क्लान्तिवितानतानवकृतः श्रीखण्डशैलानिलाः ॥४०॥

भर्तृहरि- आर्या
प्रियपुरतो युवतीनां तावत्पदमातनोति हृदि मानः ।
भवति न यावच्चन्दनतरुसुरभिर्निर्मलः पवनः ॥४१॥

भर्तृहरि- आर्या
सहकारकुसुमकेसरनिकरभरामोदमुर्च्छितदिगन्ते ।
मधुरमधुविधुरमधुपे मधौ भवेत्कस्य नोत्कण्ठा ॥४२॥

भर्तृहरि- वसंततिलका
अच्छाच्छचन्दनरसार्द्रकरा मृगाक्ष्यो
धारागृहाणि कुसुमानि च कौमुदी च ॥
मन्दो मरुत्सुमनसः शुचि हर्म्यपृष्ठं
ग्रीष्मे मदं च मदनं च विवर्धयन्ति ॥४३॥

44.

A fragrant garland, the breeze from a fan, moonlight, pollen,
fountains, sandalwood unguent, sweet wine, clear beautiful palace roof, delicate clothes
and in the company of a lotus eyed woman.
These pleasures in the summer are only for the pious.

45.

The rainy season is like a young maiden. fragrant like the Jai flower
It increases your sensual desires,
Who will not be joyous with a such a rain shower?

46.

Dark clouds in the sky, plantain trees sprouting from the ground,
fragrant winds from *Kutaja* and *Kadamba* flowers
the paean of peacocks that is heard all over the forest.
These create longing in both the happy and sad person.

- भार्तृहरि - शिखरिणी

स्रजो हृद्यामोदा व्यजनपवनश्चन्द्रकिरणाः
परागः कासारो मलयजरसः सीधु विशदम् ।।
शुचिः सौधोत्सङ्गः प्रतनु वसनं पङ्कजदृशो
निदाघार्ता ह्येतत्सुखमुपलभन्ते सुकृतिनः ।।४४।।

वर्षाऋतु

भर्तृहरि- दोधक

तरूणीवैषोद्दीपितकामा विकसितजातीपुष्पसुगन्धिः ।
उन्नतपीनपयोधरभारा प्रावृट् कुरुते कस्य न हर्षम् ? ।। ४५।।

भर्तृहरि - मालिनी

वियदुपचितमेघं भूमयः कन्दलिन्यो
नवकुटजकदम्बामोदिनो गन्धवाहाः ।।
शिखिकुलकलकेकारावावरम्या वनान्ताः
सुखिनमुसुखिनं वा सर्वमुत्कण्ङ्यन्ति ।।४६।।

47.

Dense clouds in the sky, peacocks dancing on hills,
plantain trees creating a verdant world.
Where should a weary traveler cast his glance?

48.

Lightning dancing in the sky, the fragrance of *Ketaki*,
thunderous clouds high in the sky, the paean of playful peacocks.
How can a lonely woman with beautiful eye lashes and well versed in the arts of love
bear these on a day which excites love?

49.

Dark and dense clouds in shravana, the sky full of thunder, a rain of melting hail stones,
a beautiful streak of golden lightning.
A woman in love's longing in this situation feels both joy and sadness.

50.

To remain at home when it is raining heavily,
the embrace of a woman on the excuse of a cold day
cool winds removing the fatigue of lovemaking
even the unlucky person is fortunate under these circumstances.

भर्तृहरि- आर्या

उपरि घनं घनपटलं तिर्यग्गिरयोऽपि नर्तितमयूराः ।
क्षितिरपि कन्दलधवला दृष्टिं पथिकः क्क यापयतु? ॥४७॥

भर्तृहरि- शिखरिणी

इतो विद्युद्वल्लीविलसितमितः केतकितरोः
स्फुरद्गन्धः प्रोद्यज्जलदनिनदस्फुर्जितमितः ॥
इतः केकीक्रीडाकलकलरवः पक्ष्यलदृशां
कथं यास्यन्त्येते विरहदिवसाः संभृतरसाः? ॥४८॥

भर्तृहरि- शिखरिणा

असूचीसंचारे तमसि नभसि प्रौढजलद-
ध्वनिप्राये तस्मिन् पतति दृशदां नीरनिचये ॥
इदं सौदामिन्याः कनककमनीयं विलसितं
मुदं च गलानिं च प्रथयति पथिष्वेव सुदृशाम् ॥४९॥

भर्तृहरि- शार्दूलविक्रीडित

आसारेषु न हर्म्यतः प्रिततमैर्यातुं यदा शक्यते
शीतोत्कम्पनिमित्तमायतदृशा गाढं समालिङ्ग्यते ॥
जाताः शीकरशीतलाश्च मरुतश्चात्यन्तखेदच्छिदो
धन्यानां बत दुर्दिनं सुदिनतां याति प्रियासङ्गमे ॥५०॥

51.

Fortunate are those who having slept half the night
can drink cool water mixed with autumnal moonlight
on the roof of a palace, offered by languid hands
when the body is exhausted after love making in the middle of the night
when the intoxication of wine still persists and the mouth is dry with thirst.

52.

Fortunate is the man who can rest happily in the autumn season
having eaten curd, milk and ghee, wearing red clothes, applying an unguent of saffron,
tired after many love games, embraced in his bedroom
by a sensuous woman with voluptuous breasts and hips
their mouth filled with betel

53.

In a season where the mature Priyangu blossoms,
where the bees are intoxicated with the fragrance of the Kunda flower,
where tall Mandara trees flourish on account of cool winds,
at such a time if a doe eyed woman adept in matters of love does not embrace a man
and give him warmth,
it is as if such a man suffers endless nights
and is condemned to the world of Yama.

भर्तृहरि- स्रग्धरा

अर्धे नीत्वा (किंवा सुप्त्वा) निशायाः
सरभससुरतायासखिन्नश्लथाङ्गः
प्रोदभूतासह्यतृषो मधुमदनिरतो हर्म्यपृष्ठे विविक्ते ॥
संभोगाक्लान्तकान्ताशिथिलभुजलताऽऽवर्जितं कर्करीतो
ज्योत्स्नाभिन्नाच्छधारं न पिवति सलिलं शारदं मन्दभाग्यः ॥५१॥

हेमन्तऋतु

भर्तृहरि- शार्दूलविक्रीडित

हेमन्ते दधिदुग्धसर्पिरशना माञ्जिष्ठवासोभृतः
काश्मीरद्रवसान्द्रदिग्धवपुषः खिन्ना विचित्रै रतैः ॥
पीनोरुस्तनकामिनीजनकृताश्लेषा गृहाभ्यन्तरे
ताम्बूलीदलपूगपुरितमुखा धन्याः सुखं शेरते ॥५२॥

भर्तृहरि- स्रग्धरा

प्रोद्यत्पौढप्रियङ्गुद्युतिभृति विदलत्कुन्दमाद्यद्द्विरेफे
काले प्रालेयवातप्रचलविकसितोद्दाममन्दारदाम्नि ॥
येपां नो कण्ठलग्ना क्षणमपि तुहिनक्षोददक्षा मृगाक्षी
तेपामायामयामा यमसदनसमा यामिनी याति यूनाम् ॥५३॥

54.

The winter wind caresses the cheeks of a woman, makes the hair on her face flutter,
causing sighing breaths, and makes the unclothed breasts shiver,
shaking the buttocks
and causes the waist cloth to drop.
Wintry winds play the part of lovers in broad daylight.

55.

The winter wind behaves like the beloved
who dishevels her hair,
makes her close her eyes, forcibly pulls her clothes, creates horripilation,
makes her tremble and sigh and causes sore lips.

56.

A woman haltingly goes through the trees of the forest
raising her odhni to expose her breasts as if she was exposing them to moonlight.

शिशिरऋत

भर्तृहरि- स्त्रग्धरा

चुम्बतो गण्डभित्तीरलकवति मुखे सीत्कृतान्यादधाना
वक्षःसूत्कञ्चुकेषु स्तनभरपुलकोभ्देदमापादयन्तः ॥
ऊरूनाकम्पयन्तः पृथुजघनतटात्स्रंसयन्तोंऽशुकानि
व्यक्तं कान्ताजनानां विटचरितकृतः शैशिरा वान्ति वाताः ॥५४॥

भर्तृहरि- शार्दूलविक्रीडित

केशानाकुलयन् दृशो मुकुलयन् वासो वलादाक्षिपन्
आतन्वन् पुलकोद्गमं प्रकटयन्नावेहकम्पं गतैः ॥
वारंवारमुदारसीत्कृतकृतो दन्तच्छदान्पीडयन्
प्रायः शैशिर एष सम्प्रति मरुत्कान्तासु कान्तायते ॥५५॥

रतिक्रीडा- रतिपूर्ति

भर्तृहरि- उपजाति

विश्रम्य विश्रम्य वनद्रुमाणां छायासु तन्वी विचचार हाचित् ।
स्तनोत्तरीयेण करोद्धृतेन निवारयन्ती शशिनो मखूयान् ॥५६॥

57.

A doe eyed woman who is sweet and eager for love
bending languorously, of playful speech, flirtatious, innocent
and who invokes Madana with sweet words spoken in a isolated place
can enslave any man.

58.

As long as one has not met a sensuous women one wishes to see her.
After seeing her, one wishes the joy of a loving embrace.
After the embrace, one wishes that their bodies become one.

59.

On her hair a garland of malati flowers,
on her body a paste of saffron and sandalwood,
with the beloved on his chest.
On account of this it seems as if heaven is here.

भर्तृहरि- हरिणी
प्रणयमधुरा: प्रेमोद्गाढा रसादलसास्ततो
भणितिमधुरा मुग्धप्राया: प्रकाशितसंमदा: ।।
प्रकृतिसुभगा विश्रम्भार्हा: स्मरोदयदायिनो
रहसि किमपि स्वैरालापा हरन्ति मृगीदृशाम् ।।५७।।

भर्तृहरि- उपजाति
अदर्शने दर्शनमात्रकामा
दृष्टा परिष्वङ्गसुखैकलोला: ।।
आलिङ्गितायां पुनरायताक्ष्या-
माशास्महे विग्रहयोरभेदम् ।।५८।।

भर्तृहरि- रथोध्दता
मालती शिरसि जृम्भणोन्मुखी
चन्दनं वपुषि कुङ्कुमान्वितम् ।।
वक्षसि प्रियतमा मनोहरा
स्वर्ग एव परिशिष्ट आगत: ।।५९।।

60.

In the beginning (when she was immature) as she was unaware of love sports
she would decline to participate.
But gradually she starts longing for it.
Then coyly she bashfully loosens her body
In the secluded (*pranay mandapa*) she actually embraces her beloved
and gives more pleasure in the love sport.
It is indeed a pleasure to engage with such a woman of noble lineage.

61.

Fortunate is the person who is able to drink the nectar (of her lips) from a woman
whose hair is disheveled as she lies on his chest, with half open eyes
tired after her love sport and on whose cheek there is a drop of sweat.

62.

Even Brahma cannot stop a woman who acts when she is intoxicated with love.

63.

When a couple at the end of love making
done with mutual pleasure
look at each other with half closed eyes
they experience the height of amorous pleasure.

भर्तृहरि- शार्दुलविक्रीडित

प्राङ् मनागनागतरसं जाताभिलापं ततः
सव्रीडं तदनु श्लथीकृततनु प्रध्वस्तधैर्य पुनः ॥
प्रेमांर्द स्पृहणीयनिर्भररहः क्रीडाप्रगल्भं ततो
निःशङ्काङ्गविकर्षणाधिकसुखं रम्यं कुलस्त्रीरतम् ॥६०॥

भर्तृहरि- मालिनी

उरसि निपतितानां स्त्रस्तधम्मिल्लकानां
मुकुलितनयनानां किञ्चिदुन्मीलितानाम् ॥
उपरिसुरतखेदस्विन्नगण्डस्थलीना-
मधरमधु वधूंना भाग्यवन्तः पिबन्ति ॥६१॥

भर्तृहरि- अनुष्टभ्

उन्मत्तप्रीमसंरम्भादारभन्ती यदङ्गनाः ।
तत्रप्रत्यूहमाधातुं ब्रह्माऽपि खलु कातरः ॥६२॥

भर्तृहरि- आर्या

आमीलितनयनानां यत्सुरतरसोऽनु संविदं भाति ।
मिथुनैर्मिथोऽवधारितमवितथमिदमेव कामनिर्वहणम् ॥६३॥

64.

Fortunate is the man fatigued after the pleasures of love
who can spend the night embraced by his beloved
and who places his chest upon her expansive breasts
large as an intoxicated elephant and wet with the paste of *kumkum*.

65.

When during sexual activity the minds
of the lover and beloved also become one
then the pleasures of love are complete.
When the mind is distracted
it is as if it is a union of two dead bodies.

66.

What should the learned persons having given up jealousy
say to the common person?
Should they give up this world
or spend amorous pleasures with a sensuous woman
of voluptuous breasts and buttocks?

भतृहरि - वसंततिलका
मत्तेभकुम्भपरिणाहिनि कुङ्कुमार्द्रे
कान्तापयोधरतटे रसखेदखिन्नः ।।
वक्षो निधाय भुजपञ्जरमध्यवर्ती
धन्यः क्षपां क्षपयति क्षणलब्धनिद्रः ।।६४।।

शृंगारशतक
भतृहरि- अनुष्टभ्
एतत्कामफलं लोके यद्द्वयोरेकचित्तता ।
अन्यचित्तकृते कामे शवयोरेव सङ्गमः ।।६५।।

भर्तृहरि- उपजाति
मात्सर्यमुत्सार्य विचार्य कार्य-
मार्या समर्यादमिदं वदन्तु ।।
सेव्या नितम्बाः किमु भुधराणा-मुत स्मरस्मेरविलासिनीनाम् ।।६६।।

67.

Live either in the sacred waters of the Ganga
or stay clasped to the necklace
on the breasts of a young beautiful woman.

68.

When the hearts of lovers are in unison even though they are apart from each other
they are still to be considered as enjoying each other's company.
On the contrary when there is disagreement between them
their actual company is even more painful than separation.

69.

Either you feed green delicate kusa grass to the deer
obtained by cutting the bamboo with a sharp stone
or feed your beloved the leaves of the pale green
and delicate leaves of betel creeper
soft as the light green cheek of a female parrot
plucked with your red nails.

ल.गो. विंझे- अनुष्टभ्
रहावें एक गंगेच्या पापनाशी जलान्तरीं ॥
हारें सुंदर ऐशा वा तरुनीच्या स्तनांतरी ॥६७॥

भर्तृहरि- आर्या
विरहोऽपि सङ्गमः खलु परस्परं मनो येषाम् ।
हृदयमपि विघट्टितं चेत्सङ्गो विरहं विशेषयति ॥६८॥

भर्तृहरि- मालिनी
दिश वनहरिणीभ्यः स्निग्धवंशाच्छवीनां
कवलमुपलकोटिच्छिन्नमुलं कुशानाम् ॥
शुकयुवतिकपोलापाण्डु ताम्बूलवल्ली-
दलमरुणनखाग्रैः पातितं वा वधूभ्यः ॥६९॥

70.

In this meaningless and chaotic world the wise person has only two paths.
The first path is to drink the nectar of knowledge and experience brahmananda.
The other path is to spend time with
a full breasted woman with beautiful thighs
with her hand held to protect her modesty.

71.

You may be a follower of Vedantins but we admire poets who create different kinds of poetry.
For us there is no higher merit in this world than healing others
and nothing is more beautiful than a lotus eyed woman.

72.

What use is there of useless words without reason?
There are two things worth doing (in this life).
Either enjoy the youth of a full breasted woman
or go the forest.

कविभर्तृहरिरचित शतकत्रयी

भर्तृहरि- स्रग्धरा

संसारेऽस्मिन्नसारे परिणतितरले द्वे गती पण्डितानां
तत्वज्ञानामृताम्भःप्लवलुलितधियां यातु कालः कथञ्चित् ।।
नोचेमुग्धाङ्गनानां स्तनजघनभराभोगसंभोगिनीनां
स्थुलोपस्थस्थलीषु स्थगितकरतलस्पर्शलीलोद्यतानाम् ।।७०।।

शृंगारशतक

भर्तृहरि- शिखरिणा

भवन्तो वेदान्तप्रणिहितधियामाप्तगुरवो
विचित्रालापानां वयमपि कवीनामनुचराः ।।
तथाप्येतद् ब्रूमो न हि परहितात्पुण्यमधिकं
न चास्मिन्संसारे कुवलयदृशो रम्यमपरम् ।। ७१ ।।

भर्तृहरि- मालिना

किमिह वहुभिरुक्तैर्युक्तिशून्यैः प्रलपे-
र्द्वयमिह पुरुषाणां सर्वदा सेवनीयम् ।।
अभिनवमदलीलालालसं सुंदरीणां
स्तनभरपरिखिन्नं यौवनं व वनं वा ।।७२।।

73.

Youth is the hall mark of love, a home of irrelevance
It can cause the sorrow of a hundred hells.
It is the cause of delusion, it is a cloud that obscures the moonlight of knowledge
it is the only friend of Madana, like faulty poetry, the home of anarchy.

74.

Like a cloud for the tree of love
a river of delicate playfulness
a close friend of Madana
an ocean full of pearls of trickery
eyes of a young woman like the moon for the chakor
and the natal home of a married woman.
Blessed is the person who is not disturbed by all this.

75

O King! No one has been able to cross the ocean of thirst
What use is there if one has a lot wealth
but the body and its youthful love has vanished?
It is better to go to one's home before
the beauty of one's beloved is destroyed by old age .

विषयविभाग- (ई) यौवन अनर्थकारक
भर्तृहरि- स्त्रग्धरा

रागस्यागारमेकं नरकशतमहादुःखसम्प्राप्तिहेतु-
र्मोहस्योत्पत्तिबीजं जलधरपटलं ज्ञानताराधिपस्य ॥
कन्दर्पस्यैकमित्रं प्रकटितविविधस्पष्टदोषप्रबन्धं
लोकेऽस्मिन्न ह्यनर्थव्रजकुलभवनं यौवनादन्यदस्ति ॥७३॥

कविभर्तृहरिरचित शतकत्रयी
भर्तृहरि - शार्दूलविक्रिडित

शृङ्गारद्रुमनीरदे प्रसृमरक्रीडारस स्त्रोतसि
प्रद्युम्नप्रियबान्धवे चतुरतामुक्ताफलोदन्वति ॥
तन्वीनेत्रचकोरपार्वणिविधौ सौभाग्यलक्ष्मीनिधौ
धन्यः कोऽपि न विक्रियां कलयति प्राप्ते नवे यौवने ॥७४॥

शृंगारशतक
भर्तृहरि- स्त्रग्धरा

राजंस्तृष्णाम्बुराशेर्न हि जगति गतः कश्चिदेवावसानं
को वार्थोऽर्थैः प्रभूतैः स्ववपुषि गलिते यौवने सानुरागे ॥
गच्छामः सद्म तावद्विकसितकुमुदेन्दीवरालोकिनीनां
यावच्चाक्रम्य रूपं झटिति न जरया लुप्यते प्रयसीनाम् ॥७५॥

76.

Which wise person can love the courtesan
who severs her connection with the creeper of discrimination,
sells her body for a paltry sum to a person
who is born blind, of foul mouth, old and senile, rustic,
of low birth and having a contagious disease?

77.

A person hungry for sensual pleasures
offers his youth and wealth to a woman (courtesan)
who inflames his heart with her beauty.

78.

Would a person of noble descent
kiss a woman who has become
a spittoon for a spy, robber, actor, warrior or a debauch?

विषयविभाग (उ) वेश्यानिंदा

भर्तृहरि- शार्दूलविक्रीडित

जान्त्यन्धाय च दुर्मुखाय च जराजीर्णाखिलाङ्गाय च
ग्रामीणाय च दुष्कुलाय च गलत्कुष्ठाभिभूताय च ॥
यच्छन्तीषु मनोहरं निजवपुर्लक्ष्मीलवाकाङ्क्षया
पण्यस्त्रीषु विवेककल्पलतिकाशस्त्रीपु रज्येत कः ? ॥७६॥

भर्तृहरि- अनुष्टभ्

वेश्याऽसौ मदनज्वाला रूपेन्धनविवर्धिता ।
कामिभिर्यव हूयन्ती यांवनानि धनानि च ॥७७॥

भर्तृहरि- आया

कश्चुम्बति कुलपुरूषो वेश्याधरपल्लवं मनोज्ञमपि ।
चारभटचौरचेटकनटविटनिष्ठीवनशरावम् ? ॥७८॥

79.

In this banal world without a lotus eyed woman who is radiant like the rising moon
whose waist ornament makes sweet sounds and
who is bent over with weight of her breasts
why would a noble person serve a ordinary king
with the expectation of money (which he would need to pay a courtesan)?

80.

If there were no doe eyed women who are like the weapons of Madana
would a proud person bend his head in shame?
Else they would have gone to the Himalayas
which is blessed with sages living in its valleys,
where the shoulder of Nandi bull marks the trunk of trees
where stones are washed by the spray of Ganga.

81.

If women with intoxicated eyes were not in our life
if would have been easy to cross the ocean of life.

विषयविभाग (ऊ) स्त्रीनिंदा-स्त्रीपायींच पुरूष सेवाधर्मातले अपमान गिळतो.

भर्तृहरि- स्त्रग्धरा

संसारेऽस्मिन्नसारे कुनृपतिभवनद्वासेवावलम्ब-
व्यासङ्गध्वस्तधैर्य कथममलधियो मानसं संविदध्युः? ॥
यद्येताःप्रोद्यदिन्दुद्युतिनिवयभृतो न स्युरम्भोजनेत्राः
प्रेङ्खत्काञ्चीकलापाः स्तनभरविनमन्मध्यभाजस्तरुण्यः? ॥७९॥

भर्तृहरि - शार्दूलविक्रीडित

सिद्धाध्यासितकन्दरे हरवृपस्कन्धावरुग्णद्रुमे
गङ्गाधौतशिलातले हिमवतः स्थाने स्थिते श्रेयसि ॥
कः कुर्वीत शिरः प्रणाममलिनं म्लानं मनस्वी जनो
यद्वित्रस्तकुरङ्गशावनयना न स्युः स्मरास्त्रं स्त्रियः ॥८०॥

भर्तृहरि- अनुष्टभ्

संसार ! तव निस्तार-
(किंवा संसारोदधिनिस्तार-)
पदवी न दवीयसी ।
अन्तरा दुस्तरा न स्यु-
र्यदि रे मदिरेक्षणाः ॥८१॥

82.

Without prejudice I say the truth which is true in the seven worlds
that there is nothing more alluring than a sensuous woman
and there is no greater cause of misery than a woman.

83.

A woman is called a loving wife, lotus eyed, large hipped, voluptuous,
of eloquent speech, with beautiful eyebrows.
Even a wise person seeing such a woman
becomes eager, intoxicated, pleased and engages amorously and praises her.
Truly to be deluded by a woman leads to bad outcomes.

84.

How can one call a woman virtuous
when even thinking of her creates anguish
seeing her creates lust, being touched by her creates delusion?

85.

Strange are the tricks of a woman.
As long as a man is in the company of a woman she is like nectar
but as soon as he moves away she is like poison (because he longs to see her again).

भर्तृहरि- इद्रवज्रा

सत्यं जना वच्मि न पक्षपाताल्लोकेषु सप्तस्वपि तथ्यमेतत् ।
नान्यन्मनोहारि नितम्बिनीभ्यो दुःखैकहेतुर्न च कश्चिदन्यः ॥८२॥

भर्तृहरि- शार्दूलविक्रीडित

कान्तेत्युत्पललोचनेति विपुलश्रोणीभरेत्युत्सुकः
पीनोत्तुङ्गपयोधरेति सुमुखाम्भोजेति सुभ्रूरिति ॥
दृष्टा माद्यति मोदतेऽभिरमते प्रस्तौति विद्वानपि
प्रत्यक्षाशुचिभस्त्रिकां स्त्रियनहो मोहस्य दुश्चेष्टितम् ॥८३॥

भर्तृहरि- अनुष्टम्

स्मृता भवति तापाय दृष्टा चोन्मादवर्धिनी ।
स्पृष्टा भवति मोहाय ! सा नाम 'दयिता' कथम् ? ॥८४॥

भर्तृहरि - अनुष्टभ्

तावदेवामृतमयी यावल्लोचनगोचरा ।
चक्षुःपथादतीता तु विषदप्यतिरिच्यते ॥८५॥

86.

A woman is both poison and nectar.
As long as she loves you she is like nectar.
As soon as she stops loving her she is a creeper of poison.

87.

This world is like a whirl full of suspicion (vortex), a home of insults,
a city of bravado, a treasure of faults, a place of hundred deceits,
a field of broken loyalty, an obstacle to the door of heaven,
the entry door of hell, where delusions resides.
Who created a tricky woman who is full of nectar and poison
who can trap living beings (in this world)?

88.

Poets have created an imaginary woman with her face like the moon,
eyes like the lotus and a golden body.
Knowing this only a fool will adore a woman's skin, flesh and bones.

भर्तृहरि- अनुष्टभ्
नामृतं न विषं किञ्चिदेकां मुक्त्वा नितम्बिनीम् ।
सैवामृतरुता रक्ता विरक्ता विषवल्लरी ॥८६॥

भर्तृहरि- स्त्रग्धरा
आवर्तः संशयानामविनयभवनं पत्तनं साहसानां
दोषाणां संविधानं कपटशतमयं क्षेत्रमप्रत्ययानाम् ॥
स्वर्गदारस्य विघ्नौ नरकपुरमुखं सर्वमायाकरण्डं
स्त्रीयन्त्रं केन सृष्टं विषममृतमयं प्राणिलोकस्य पाशः ॥८७॥

भर्तृहरि- शार्दूलविक्रीडित
नो सत्येन मृगाङ्क एष वदनीभूतो न चेन्दीवर-
द्वन्द्वं लोचनतां गतं, न कनकैरप्यङ्गयष्टि कृता ॥
किं त्वेवं कविभिः प्रतारितमनास्तत्वं विज्ञानन्नपि
त्वङ्मांसास्थिमयं वपुर्मृगदृशां मन्दो जनः सेवते ॥८८॥

89.

Romantic gestures are a natural expression of a young woman.
Foolish men feel that these are meant for them and get attracted towards them.
The red colour is the natural colour of the lotus however the bee feels it is to attract them.

90.

The lotus face of a young woman is truly beautiful
rivaling the splendour of the full moon
in her lips is nectar
Once this has passed like the fruit of a tree
it becomes lifeless and like poison and a source of sorrow.

91.

Just as it is difficult to touch a reflection in the mirror
it is difficult to find the heart of a woman.
Just as the winding, tangled and narrow roads in a mountain
the feelings of a woman are difficult to feel or understand.
The wise have said that the mind of a woman is like drops of water on a lotus leaf
in short like the blossoms of a poison creeper the faults of a woman only increase.

भर्तृहरि- उपजाति

लीलावतीनां सहजा विलासा-
स्त एव मूढस्य हृदि स्फुरन्ति ॥
रागो नलिन्या हि निसर्गसिद्ध-
स्तत्र भ्रमत्येव वृथा षडङ्घ्रिः ॥८९॥

भर्तृहरि- शिखरिणी

यदेतत्पूर्णेन्दुद्युतिहरमुदाराकृतिवरं
मुखाब्जं तन्वङ्ग्याः किल वसति तत्राधरमधु ॥
इदं तत्किम्पाकद्रुमफलमिवातीव विरसं
व्यतीतेऽस्मिन् काले विषमिव भविष्यत्यसुखदम् ॥९०॥

भर्तृहरि- शार्दूलविक्रीडित

अग्राह्यं हृदयं यथैव वदनं यद्दर्पणान्तर्गतं
भावः पर्वतसुक्ष्ममार्गविषमः स्त्रीणां न विज्ञायते ।.
चित्तं पुष्करपत्रतोयतरलं विद्वद्भिराशंसितं
नारी नाम विषाङ्कुरैरिव लता दोषैः समं वर्धिता ॥९१॥

92.

One cannot trust a woman
she will chat with one
look at another flirtatiously
and think of yet another.
Who does she really love?

93.

There is nectar in a young woman's mouth
but deadly poison in her heart
that is why her lips are sucked
and rub their breasts with their fist.

94.

O lustful man!
Melodious songs, sensuous dance, sweet juice of the lips,
fragrance of the mouth, exciting touch of the breasts.
Your selfish five senses will deceive you and will destroy your destiny.

भर्तृहरि- अनुष्टभ्
जल्पन्ति सार्धमन्येय पश्यन्त्यन्यं सविभ्रमम् ।
हृद्गतं चिन्तयन्त्यन्यं प्रियः को नाम योषिताम् ? ॥९२॥

भर्तृहरि- वैतालीय
मधु तिष्ठति वाचि योषितां हृदि हालाहलमेव केवलम् ॥
अत एव निपीयतेऽधरो हृदयं मुष्टिभिरेव ताड्यते ॥९३॥

भर्तृहरि- मालिनी
इह हि मधुरगीतं नृत्यमीतद्रसोऽयं
स्फुरति परिमलोऽसौ स्पर्श एप स्तनानाम।
इति हतपरमार्थैरिन्द्रियैर्भ्राम्यमाणः
स्वहितकरणदक्षैः पञ्चभिर्वञ्चितोऽसि ॥९४॥

95.

Even a man proficient in the scriptures, knowledgeable in ethics and self-realised
will rarely finds the right path in this transient world
because a woman with side long glances and dancing eye brows
holds a key to the netherworld.

96.

A woman's body with three folds around her waist is like a dangerous river
with voluptuous breasts like the two *chakravaka* birds and her lotus face.
If you do not want to drown in it stay away from her.

97.

Friend! Stay away from a woman who is like a snake
whose side long glances are like poison
whose playfulness is like the hood whose behavior is insincere.
There is a remedy for a snake bite
but not for one who has been afflicted by a woman
for even a physician will give up.

भर्तृहरि- मंदाक्रांता

शास्त्रज्ञोऽपि प्रथितविनयोऽप्यात्तबोधोऽपि वाढं
संसारेऽस्मिन्भवति विरलो भाजनं सद्गतीनाम् ॥
येनैतस्मिन्निरयनगरद्वारमुद्घाटयन्ती
वामाक्षीणा भवति कुटिला भ्रूलता कुञ्चिकेव ॥९५॥

विषयविभाग- (ए) उपरतीचा प्रारंभ

भर्तृहरि- शार्दूलविक्रीडित

उन्मीलत्त्रिवलीतरङ्गनिलया प्रोत्तुङ्गपीनस्तन-
द्वन्द्वेनोद्यतचक्रवाकमिथुना वक्त्राम्बुजोद्भासिनी ॥
कान्ताकारधरा नदीयमभितः क्रूराशया नेष्यते
संसारार्णवमज्जनं यदि तदा दूरेण सन्त्यज्यताम् ॥९६॥

भर्तृहरि - हरिणी

अपसर सखे दूरादस्मात्कटाक्षविषानलात्
प्रकृतिकुटिलाद्योपित्सर्पाद्विलासफणाभृतः ॥
इतरफणिना दष्टः शक्यश्चिकित्सितुमौषधै-
श्चतुरवनिताभोगिग्रस्तं त्यजन्ति हि मन्त्रिणः ॥९७॥

98.

Even when a person gets old and is still afflicted by Madana it is not natural or appropriate.
When a woman has sagging breasts she should desist from romantic activity
as it not proper for her to do so.

99.

Lucky is the person who is not attracted to a woman
with large and restless eyes
firm and youthful breasts, with creeper like folds above a slender waist.

100.

When I was under the influence of love I saw the whole world as full of women.
Now having applied the corryllium of knowledge to my eyes
I have regained perfect vision and look on all things alike
and feel the presence of Brahman in the three worlds.

भर्तृहरि-पुष्पिताग्रा
इदमनुचितमकमश्च पुंसां
यदहि जरास्वपि मान्मथा विकाराः ।
यदपि च न कृतं नितम्बिनीनां
सतनपतनावधि जीवितं रतं वा ।।९८।।

भर्तृहरि - वसंततिलका
धन्यास्त एव तरलायतलोचनानां
तारुण्यदर्पघन पीनपयोधराणाम् ।।
क्षामादरोपरिलसत्त्रिवलीलतानां
दृष्टाऽऽकृतिं विकृतिमेति मनो न येषाम् ।।९९।।

भर्तृस्ज्;हरि -शिखरिणी
यदाऽसीदशानं स्मरतिमिरसञ्चारजनितं
तदा सर्वे नारीमयमिदमर्शेट्;ां जगदभूत् ।
इदानीमस्माकं पटुतरविवेकाञ्चनदृशां
समीभता दृष्टिस्त्रिभुवनमपि ब्रह्म मनुते ।।१००।।

Vidai

Aravinda Rao

शृङ्गारार्णव-मज्जनातुरतया भ्रान्तं मदीयं मनः
काव्ये भर्तृहरेः अजेयसुरतास्फोटादि रङ्गस्थले।
वैराग्याख्य-कशाभिघात-चकितं मनो-जृंभणम्
शृङ्गाराब्धि-रसाभिषेक-मिषया वैराग्य-मुज्जृंभते।।

My mind reached out to the *kavya* of Bhartrhari to dive into the ocean of *shringara*
A *kavya* which is the arena of amorous fights where there is no winner
My restless mind was silenced by the whip of *vairagya*
On the pretext of the *abhisheka* of *shringara rasa vairagya* ultimately prevailed.

Authors

Harsha V. Dehejia has a double doctorate, one in Medicine and the other in Ancient Indian Culture, both from Mumbai University. He divides his time between Ottawa, Canada and Mumbai, India. He is a practising Physician and Adjunct Professor of Religion in the College of Humanities of CarletonUniversity in Ottawa. His main interest is in Krishna Shringara in which subject he has more than 25 books, two films and many curated exhibitions.

Narmada Prasad Upadhyaya is a noted scholar of Hindi literature and Indian Painting. Among his books on Indian painting are, Bhartiya Chitrankan Prampara (Hindi), Paar Roop Ke (Hindi), Jain Chitrankan Parampara (Hindi), Kanheri Geet Govinda Paintings in Kanheri style, The Concept of Portrait in the Context of Indian Miniature Paintings, The Color's Fragrance, Paintings of Bundelkhand ,Some Remembered, Some Forgotten, Some Not Yet Discovered (with Dr. Harsha Dehejia) and Amarukshataka, A Centennial of Love Songs (with Dr. Harsha Dehejia). He was awarded the Kala Bhushan in 2003 and the Sharad Joshi Award for Lalit Nibandha.

Dr. Aravinda Rao was a distinguished Police Officer but later distinguished himself in Sanskrit obtaining a doctorate from the Telugu University Hyderabad. He has numerous books in English and Telegu on Vedanta. He was awarded the title Vachaspati by the Rashtirya Sanskrita Vidya Peeth, Tirupati and Samskrita Deva Vrata by the Rashtriya Samskita Samsthan, Delh